THE
APOCALYPSE
HAS BEGUN

THE
APOCALYPSE
HAS BEGUN

STEVE TERRELL

REDEMPTION⬥PRESS

Published by Redemption Press, PO Box 427, Enumclaw, WA 98022

ISBN 13: 978-1-63232-102-2
Library of Congress Catalog Card Number: 2009904997

CONTENTS

ACKNOWLEDGMENTS

There are many people who have helped, made suggestions, edited, proof read, and encouraged me along the long road to this completed manuscript. They have been His conduits. With deep gratitude I thank them all.

However, my desire is that the focus of honor, gratitude, and thanks be to the real source of the book: The Living God. To Him this book is humbly dedicated.

INTRODUCTION

Some years ago, I was introduced to the late Pastor Charles F. Noble of Mina, Nevada. He had developed a thesis that the four beasts of Daniel 7 were not ancient empires but modern nations. The thoughts of contemplating such an idea lay dormant with me for a number of years, because at the time I was a dyed-in-the-wool pretribulationist, and this thesis just didn't fit into my scheme of end-times thinking.

One day I took his book *Drama of the Ages* off the shelf and gave his thesis a second look. For better or for worse, this started my journey of thinking outside of the box. *Were the nineteenth and twentieth century eschatology expositors mistaken about the four beasts of Daniel 7? If so, could they have missed other prophetic events?* At that point, I began to question everything I had ever read regarding the end times.

By the time Marvin Rosenthal's book *The Pre-Wrath Rapture of the Church* came out in 1990, I had taken the position of a "three-and-one-half year tribulationist," because I could find no Scriptural basis for seven years of tribulation. Rosenthal's thesis regarding the rapture was the final element that made a cohesive whole out of the end-times pieces that I had been gathering.

I am convinced that the nineteenth and twentieth century Bible scholars were attempting, to the best of their understanding and knowledge, to interpret the Scriptures correctly. However, they were at a tremendous disadvantage when they wrote their major works on eschatology. They were attempting to interpret the book of Daniel before it had been "unsealed" in 1948—the year that Israel, God's Scriptural timepiece, was reborn as a sovereign nation after approximately 2,500 years of being scattered throughout the Gentile nations. This "rebirth" was also the event that marked the beginning of the "time of the end."

Unfortunately, the misconceptions made by these Christian scholars have remained as major premises in the modern American evangelical end-times belief system. The following are just a few of the questionable positions they have presented regarding the end times:

- The rapture (the time when believing Christians will be caught up into heaven) will take place sometime before the opening of the last seven years of this age.
- The identity of the Beast of Daniel and Revelation will not be revealed until after the church has been raptured.
- The man called the Antichrist/Beast will come on the scene during the beginning of the last seven years and will somehow convince the nations of the world to form a one-world government over which he will rule.
- This despotic world ruler will receive a mortal head wound and then be resurrected.

If you have problems connecting the dots in this end-times picture, and if you also have a nagging feeling that something is missing, but you don't know exactly what it is, then I invite you to read on.

My purpose in writing *The Apocalypse Has Begun* is not to offer an exhaustive compilation of end times events, because I don't in any way pretend to have all the answers. Rather, I humbly hope to submit for your consideration my ideas and biblical research as small steps in the right direction for establishing a clearer view of God's great plan for the end of the age, so that the world might be warned even as it was warned by Noah.

CHAPTER 1

THE FOURTH BEAST OF THE APOCALYPSE

Like the undetected flight of a stealth fighter plane, the beginning of the Apocalypse slipped in past the ever-vigilant aficionados of eschatology silently and unseen. It began with the birth of the European Single Market on December 31, 1992, an event that fulfilled the prophecy given in Revelation 17:12: "The ten horns you saw are ten kings who have not yet received a kingdom, but who for one hour will receive authority as kings along with the beast." Jacques Delors, who was president of the Commission of the European Union (EU) at the time, received this kingdom along with the ten nations when the European Single Market was created in 1992.

The second event of the Apocalypse will take place during 2014 when the EU will move into fiscal and political union. At the same time they are expected to appoint Jacques Delors as the first and last president of that union. This event fulfills the prophecy given in Revelation 17:12–13 [The ten kings who received authority as kings for one hour along with the beast] … "will give their power and authority to the beast." The new president will not take this authority by force, as so many prophecy pundits have maintained, but will be appointed to the position.

How the Ten Nations Evolved

From its very beginning in 1950, prophecy experts have been looking at the EU as a possible revival of the old Roman Empire as foretold in the book of Daniel. This concept of the EU is based on a dream of Nebuchadnezzar, king of Babylon, as recorded in Daniel 2.

Nebuchadnezzar's Babylonian kingdom was the first great power of the biblical period known as "the times of the Gentiles" (see Luke 21:24). This biblical period began in 586 B.C., when Nebuchadnezzar invaded Israel, destroyed the Temple (the center of Jewish worship), and deported the Jews to Babylon.

In his dream, Nebuchadnezzar saw a huge, poly-metallic image of a man. The image had a head made of gold, chest and arms made of silver, and a belly and thighs made of bronze. The legs were made of iron, and the feet were iron mixed with clay. Then a stone came out of heaven and crushed the toes of the image, and the whole image collapsed and was blown away in the wind.

Nebuchadnezzar, being deeply troubled by this vision, sought the interpretation of the dream from his so-called wise men—the magicians, sorcerers, and astrologers of his court. The king insisted that the wise men give him the interpretation of his dream before he told it to them. He knew that the only way he could know their interpretation was correct was by first refusing to tell them what he had seen. The king then informed the wise men that if they didn't tell him the dream and its interpretation, they would all be put to death.

Daniel (one of the relocated Jews) was considered to be one of the wise men, because God had given him great knowledge and special understanding of literature and learning. In addition, "Daniel could understand visions and dreams of all kinds" (Dan. 1:17). Seemingly, Daniel was unaware of the decree, because when the king's guard arrived to carry him off to be killed with the other wise men, Daniel asked the guard what the problem was. When the guard told him about the king's decree, Daniel went to the king and asked him for a little time so that he, Daniel, might interpret the dream. The following is the interpretation of the dream that God gave to Daniel to pass on to the king:

You, O king, are the king of kings. The God of heaven has given you the dominion and power and might and glory; in your hands he has placed mankind and the beasts of the field and the birds of the air. Wherever they live, he has made you ruler over them all. You are that head of gold.

After you, another kingdom will rise, inferior to yours. Next, a third kingdom, one of bronze, will rule over the whole earth. Finally, there will be a fourth kingdom, strong as iron—for iron breaks and smashes everything—and as iron breaks things to pieces, so it will crush and break all the others. Just as you saw that the feet and toes were partly of baked clay and partly of iron, so this will be a divided kingdom; yet it will have some of the strength of iron in it, even as you saw iron mixed with clay. As the toes were partly iron and partly clay, so this kingdom will be partly strong and partly brittle. And just as you saw the iron mixed with baked clay, so the people will be a mixture and will not remain united, any more than iron mixes with clay.

In the time of those kings, the God of heaven will set up a kingdom that will never be destroyed, nor will it be left to another people. It will crush all those kingdoms and bring them to an end, but it will itself endure forever. This is the meaning of the vision of the rock cut out of a mountain, but not by human hands—a rock that broke the iron, the bronze, the clay, the silver and the gold to pieces.

—Daniel 2:37–45

Daniel began the interpretation of Nebuchadnezzar's dream by telling the king that he was the head of gold he had seen in his dream. Daniel then went on to explain that the portions of the statue made of other metals represented the kingdoms that would follow Babylon in succession. In Daniel 2:38, we learn that the chest and arms of silver, the second great power, represented the Medo-Persian Empire, which conquered Babylon in 539 B.C. Then in Daniel 8:20–21, we learn that the belly and thighs of bronze represented Greece, which conquered the Medo-Persian Empire in 330 B.C. (In Daniel's prophecy, the ram, representing the kings of Media and Persia, is destroyed by a goat, representing the kingdom of Greece.) These amazing predictions could only have been God speaking through Daniel, because at the time,

Greece consisted of a number of individual city-states and was not yet known as a country. In fact, the Medes and Persians ruled over the area called Thrace for some 200 years before it became Greece.

The fourth empire, represented by the legs of iron in the dream, is unnamed in Scripture, but because it historically succeeds the Greek Empire, we have to assume that it is the Roman Empire. After the death of Alexander the Great in 323 B.C., the Greek Empire was divided among his four generals. During the next several centuries, the Roman legions gradually began to conquer the remains of Alexander's Empire, until it controlled all of the Mediterranean and most of the known world at that time. In 395 A.D., the Roman Empire was divided into an Eastern Empire and a Western Empire. The legs of iron in Nebuchadnezzar's dream represented this division. Then in 800 A.D., the Western Empire became known as the Holy Roman Empire. The Pope took over the reins of the crumbling empire and crowned Charlemagne as its emperor. This kingdom was represented by the feet of the statue that were made of clay mixed with iron.

The Western Empire did not remain united for long. Individual kingdoms began to break off from it, and by the conclusion of the Thirty Years' War in 1648, the Peace of Westphalia had given the territories in the empire almost complete independence. Then in 1806, the empire suffered what appeared to be a mortal blow when the French emperor Napoleon defeated Francis II of Austria and forced him to resign the title of Holy Roman Emperor. However, the Roman Empire continued to limp along through the years in a crippled condition, as behind the scenes the Vatican still maintained its control on the Western Empire and its people.

In Daniel 2:42–44, after the prophet describes the toes of the statue made partly of iron and partly of clay, he goes on to state, "In the times of those kings …" The kings under discussion at this point are those that make up the ten-toe kingdom and not the kings of the other metallic empires. Because the toes are connected to the legs of iron, we see that the toes represent a ten-nation confederation that will develop out of the Roman Empire.

At the end of the dream, Nebuchadnezzar sees a Rock coming out of heaven that smashes the toes of the statue, which represent the

Gentile empire of the last days. The entire statue is ground to powder and blown away in the wind. The Rock represents the Kingdom of God, which Jesus will set up at His return. He will do away with Satan's world system (the statue) and replace it with His millennial (1,000-year) reign on earth.

For approximately 2,500 years after Nebuchadnezzar conquered Israel in 586 B.C., Israel was not a sovereign nation. It wasn't until May 14, 1948, following a decision by the United Nations to create a Jewish state in Palestine, that the nation of Israel was reborn in the Promised Land (Isaiah 66:7–8). However, this event did not indicate the end of the times of the Gentiles, for those in power in Israel are still greatly influenced by their Gentile allies. In fact, the times of the Gentiles will only end when Christ's empire, defeats the forces of the Gentile empire at the battle of Armageddon, sets up His Millennial Kingdom, and collects the twelve scattered tribes from around the world.

The Horn Dilemma

According to this interpretation of the prophecy in Daniel, the ten toes are a revival of the Roman Empire. The European Union is viewed by many as that revival. But here a problem emerges, because in Revelation 17:12–13, John uses horns to describe the ten nations instead of toes. The reason for this, I believe, is because of Daniel's vision in 7:2–13, which he describes as follows:

> "In my vision at night I looked, and there before me were the four great winds of heaven churning up the great sea. Four great beasts, each different from the others, came up out of the sea.
>
> The first was like a lion, and it had the wings of an eagle. I watched until its wings were torn off and it was lifted from the ground so that it stood on two feet as a man, and a heart of a man was given to it.
>
> And there before me was a second beast, which looked like a bear. It was raised up on one of its sides, and it had three ribs in its mouth between its teeth. It was told to, "Get up and eat your fill of flesh!"
>
> After that, I looked and there before me was another beast, one that looked like a leopard. And on its back it had four wings like

those of a bird. This beast had four heads, and it was given authority to rule.

And after that, in my vision at night I looked, and there before me was a fourth beast—terrifying and frightening and very powerful. It had large iron teeth; it crushed and devoured its victims and trampled underfoot whatever was left. It was different from all the other beasts, and it had ten horns.

While I was thinking about the horns, there before me was another horn, a little one, which came up among them; and three of the first horns were uprooted before it. The horn had eyes like the eyes of a man and a mouth that spoke boastfully.

As I looked,

Thrones were set in place, and the Ancient of Days took his seat.

His clothing was white as snow; the hair of his head was white like wool.

His throne was flaming with fire, and its wheels were all ablaze.

A river of fire was flowing, coming out before him.

Thousands upon thousands attended him; ten thousand times ten thousand stood before him.

The court was seated, and the books were opened.

Then I continued to watch because of the boastful words the horn was speaking. I kept looking until the beast was slain and its body destroyed and thrown into the blazing fire. (The other beasts had been stripped of their authority, but were allowed to live for a period of time.)"

The ten horns on the fourth beast of Daniel 7 are a representation of the ten toes on the statue in Daniel 2, but they are set in different contexts. The statue represents Satan's world system, and the toes are part of that statue. The four beasts of Daniel 7, on the other hand, do not represent Satan's world system but rather four modern nations. In Daniel 7, the fourth beast is not the Old Roman Empire with its ten horns (nations) that evolve later in the last days, as many have concluded. Rather, it is the image of a revived Roman Empire featuring the ten horn nations. Because the ten horns are a revival of the Roman Empire, the Roman Empire must be seen as part of the organic whole. To picture this merger in Daniel 7 a different way, think of it as an iceberg. The Roman Empire is that part of the iceberg under the water that holds up the EU (the ten horns) above the water.

In the Beginning

On May 9, 1950, the foundation for the EU was laid when Robert Schuman, the French foreign minister, drew up a plan calling for Europe's nations to join together to exert joint control over the continent's coal and steel production, the most important materials for the armaments industry. Seven years later, in 1957, the European Common Market, as the EU was known at that time, was officially organized when six European nations joined the coalition. These nations were Germany, France, the Netherlands, Belgium, Italy, and Luxembourg. The document that drew them together was known as The Treaty of Rome.

Sixteen years later, in 1973, the United Kingdom, Denmark, and Ireland joined the European Economic Community (EEC), as the EU was known at that time. These three new members excited prophecy buffs, because they were convinced that the membership of one more nation would complete the prophesied ten nations described in Daniel 2:42–44. Greece became the tenth nation in 1981, but it soon became evident that there had to be something more cohesive among these nations than just the Common Market as it was set up at that time.

Four years later, in 1985, the catalyst for the political binding between these European nations appeared on the scene when Jacques Delors, the French Finance Minister, was appointed president of the Commission of the EEC. Delors had been a successful bank executive and an outstanding union negotiator. He made solid friendships with some of the important heads of state, which subtly enabled him to steer the EEC in the direction of a centralized government.

No Ten Horns

Expectations of a ten-nation federation evaporated in 1986 when Spain and Portugal joined the EEC, bringing the grand total of member nations to twelve. No one realized at the time that with the membership of these two nations the biblical ten horns of the last Gentile empire had been completed: "The ten horns you saw are ten kings who have not yet received a kingdom" (Rev. 17:12).

A year later, in 1987, the EEC Council of Ministers passed the Single European Act, which set an objective of establishing a European

Single Market by December 31, 1992. Under this Single Market, the member countries were to remain sovereign but appear as one nation—much like the United States of America, only without a federal government. The governing authority for the Single Market consisted of the heads of state for all twelve member nations (known as the "Council of Ministers"), with each member nation rotating in the presidency for a six-month term. This fulfilled the biblical prophecy given in Revelation 17:12, which states that these "kings without a kingdom" will receive authority as kings "for one hour" (Rev. 17:12).

The plan of the Single Market was to bring about a barrier-free Europe by December 31, 1992. Under this system, it was hoped that people, goods, money, transportation, and services would be able to move freely between the borders of all member nations. Each nation agreed to abide by some 285 physical, technical, and fiscal directives drafted by the Commission, the administrative wing of the EU located in Brussels, Belgium. These directives were an attempt to standardize the multitude of differing regulations and codes in the member countries. (If you've ever gone to Europe and tried to plug in an American electrical appliance, you're aware of the problem Europe faced in just one area of attempting to find uniformity).[1]

A Wobbly Start

The Single Market was a sure-footed step forward in the European Community's faltering march toward political union. In 1988, James M. Markham, chief of *The New York Times'* Paris bureau, wrote the following:

> Sensing a deadline of historic proportions, European Community Governments have begun intensive campaigns to alert citizens, and particularly small and medium-sized businesses of the implications of "1992"—a shorthand that has simplified the work of headline writers in a dozen languages. Already European based, multi-national businesses constitute powerful pro-1992 lobbies. While American and Japanese concerns are opening more branches here to make sure they have a foot in the door, Belgium has created a ministry to deal with 1992, and Italian television has spawned two quiz shows to sensitize the public to the rendezvous.

It is rare for a Western European politician to deliver a policy statement without dedication of a significant passage to 1992. When Prime Minister Ciriaco de Mita of Italy presented his new government's program in April, he mentioned 1992 some sixteen times, and in a spring presidential campaign in France, the leading candidates vied to show their ardor for a unified Europe.[2]

Someone once said, "The Union is like a bicycle. Unless it keeps moving, it falls over." Delors was aware that this could happen with the EU, so he and his staff produced the Maastricht Treaty, which he named for the small city of Maastricht in the Netherlands where the Council of Ministers held their summit in June of 1991. This treaty, in addition to being an adjunct to the Single Market, provided the framework for future political unification for the members of the EU. It laid the foundation for agreement on a European Monetary Union (EMU) by January 1, 1999, and it embraced the populations of the member states as citizens of the EU. The member nations were to strive toward a common defense and foreign policy. All the while, Delors kept pushing and shoving the EU towards the Single Market system.

At the time, Delors and the Commission were concerned that the treaty would not be ratified as mandated by all twelve nations. Denmark and Britain had expressed some resistance toward the more federal look of the EU, and the Commission was fearful that these two nations might cast negative votes on the treaty. If this happened, Delors and his staff would have to go back to the drawing board to rewrite the whole plan and then come back to the Council of Ministers at a later date. This was a major concern, as they had worked long and hard to prepare the document. The Council was convinced that it was now or never to move toward a more federal stance for the EU.

Between 1991 and 1992, all twelve nations signed the Maastricht Treaty. However, only *ten* nations ratified the treaty at that time. As suspected, the two flies in the ointment were Denmark and Britain. Denmark attempted to ratify the treaty in 1992, but it was not received well by its public. In Great Britain, Prime Minister John Major expressed concern that he wouldn't be able to get enough support for the treaty, and he balked at presenting it to his Parliament in 1992.

In order to prevent further delay, at the Edinburgh Summit on December 9, 1992, the Council gave Great Britain and Denmark opt-outs of certain sections of the treaty in hopes that these concessions would lead to easier ratification in those countries. Denmark was allowed to opt out from citizenship in the EU and from adopting a common European currency, defense, and foreign policy. Great Britain's opt-outs pertained to the Social Policy (which had to do with labor laws) and policies on common defense, foreign policy, and a common European currency.

With these concessions in place, all twelve countries entered the Maastricht Treaty on December 31, 1992, although Denmark and Great Britain did not ratify the treaty at that time. This finally occurred in November of 1993, when both Denmark and Britain ratified the treaty on the provision that they would be able to keep the opt-outs given to them by the other ten nations. With these items left out of their agreement to the treaty, there was not much left binding these two countries to the document. In other words, Britain and Denmark did not have the single-mindedness of the other ten nations, and in the years since, they have continued to maintain these opt-outs.

As of January 1, 1993, all passports issued in the Single Market carry the flag of the EU, and all auto license plates issued within the Union are imprinted with the EU flag. December 31, 1992 was surely the birth of something new and unparalleled in world history: twelve sovereign nations ruling over a very unique kind of country.

The Hub of the Revival

The hub of the revival of the Roman Empire was not Rome, as would have been expected, but in Brussels, Belgium. The Berlaymont building in Brussels, the capital building for the EU, houses the Commission and some 20,000 "Eurocrats" who carry on the daily activities of the EU. Those who have seen this huge, black glass building from the air often comment that it looks like a glittering five-pointed star. How appropriate for Satan, the fallen star of darkness, incarnate in the man who will be the dreaded Beast of Revelation 13 to rule from the 13th floor (the top floor) of a building with such an appearance.

The city of Brussels has had an interesting past. In 700 A.D, the people of this then-small village, prompted by their fear of Satan and his minions, elected to have the archangel, Michael, as their patron saint. They made this choice because, according to Revelation 12, Michael will cast Satan out of heaven at the beginning of the last half of the seven years of this current age. It made no difference to the people of Brussels that Michael's official position is to protect the people of Israel. They were sure they could count on Michael's watchful eye over their village.

Down through the years, many artists in Brussels have attempted to reflect this other-world conflict between Michael and Satan. One excellent example of this is a beautiful gold leaf statuary representation of Michael standing victoriously over a defeated Satan located just inside the entrance of Saint Michael's Cathedral in downtown Brussels. Another example is the townhall building, which contains a representation of a defeated Satan on the very peak of the building. To this day, the two copper figures, patina covered by years of sun and rain, can be seen on top of the townhall tower. They appear as if frozen in a future time warp against the Brussels sky, foreshadowing God's final victory over evil.

In 1695, the king of France, attempting to overrun a nearby Belgian province, tried to distract the Belgian army by attacking the city of Brussels. The king ordered his generals to place their cannons along the top of a small ridge of hills on one side of Brussels and then shelled the city continuously for forty-eight hours. At the end of the second day, the French forces had almost leveled the main part of the city. The town hall should have been obliterated, but amazingly, the structure and its tower made it through without a scratch. It was as if something or someone had protected it.

We discover in Revelation 12:7–9 that when Michael casts Satan out of heaven, Satan will find himself on the earth. He will immediately incarnate himself in the Beast, whose headquarters will probably be within the black glass Berlaymont building in the city of Brussels. As it turns out, what the early people of Brussels were trying so desperately to avoid will prove to be a viper nestled in their bosom. In the last days, Brussels will be thrust into the world spotlight when it emerges as the vortex of power for the Beast of the Apocalypse.

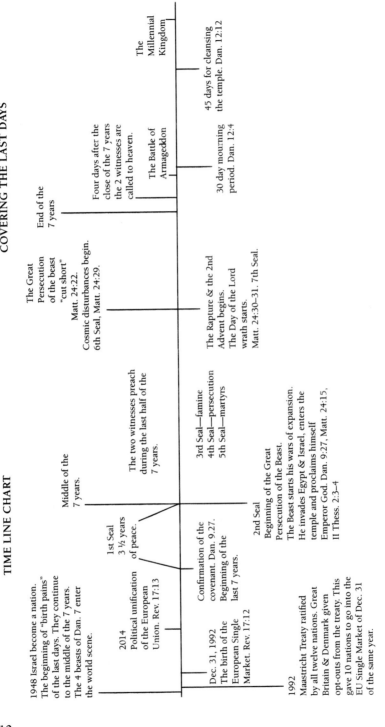

TIME LINE CHART

COVERING THE LAST DAYS

1948 Israel become a nation. The beginning of "birth pains" of the last days. They continue to the middle of the 7 years. The 4 beasts of Dan. 7 enter the world scene.

Dec. 31, 1992 The birth of the European Single Market. Rev. 17:12

1992 Maastricht Treaty ratified by all twelve nations. Great Britain & Denmark given opt-outs from the treaty. This gave 10 nations to go into the EU Single Market of Dec. 31 of the same year.

2014 Political unification of the European Union. Rev. 17:13

1st Seal 3½ years of peace.

Confirmation of the covenant. Dan. 9:27. Beginning of the last 7 years.

2nd Seal Beginning of the Great Persecution of the Beast. The Beast starts his wars of expansion. He invades Egypt & Israel, enters the temple and proclaims himself Emperor God. Dan. 9:27, Matt. 24:15, II Thess. 2:3–4

Middle of the 7 years.

The two witnesses preach during the last half of the 7 years.

3rd Seal—famine 4th Seal—persecution 5th Seal—martyrs

The Great Persecution of the beast "cut short" Matt. 24:22. Cosmic disturbances begin. 6th Seal, Matt. 24:29.

The Rapture & the 2nd Advent begins. The Day of the Lord wrath starts. Matt. 24:30–31. 7th Seal.

End of the 7 years

Four days after the close of the 7 years the 2 witnesses are called to heaven.

The Battle of Armageddon

30 day mourning period. Dan. 12:4

The Millennial Kingdom

45 days for cleansing the temple. Dan. 12:12

The Twelve Stars of the European Union

According to an article in *Europe Magazine* in 1987, the Belgians minted the first coins in the new European Currency Unit for the collector's market only. Imprinted on the coins were twelve stars, symbolizing the twelve nations of the EU, and the bust of Emperor Charles the Fifth, who was born in the Belgian town of Ghent in 1500 and was crowned the ruler of the Holy Roman Empire in 1519. According to the article, Charles the Fifth was chosen to be immortalized on the currency because of the striking geographical similarity between the Holy Roman Empire and the European Common Market.[3]

Unfortunately, despite any similarities Europeans may see between the EU and the Holy Roman Empire, the Europe of today is anything but holy. For the most part, the continent is post-Christian. Even with a population of 370 million people who claim to have a Christian heritage, most Europeans have turned their backs on the Roman Catholic Church's version of Christianity. They have relegated Christianity to the age of the dinosaurs, and this condition has led to a lack of biblical knowledge that has caused most Europeans to be blinded to the darker implications of a unified Europe. Because of this blindness and their willingness to go along with a federal Europe, they are now merging into the fast lane on the apocalyptic autobahn.

The flag of the EU is composed of a circle of twelve gold stars against a royal blue background. At the time the flag was being created, the EU intended to grow in membership; however, they decided to limit the number of stars on the flag to twelve. It's interesting to note that in Revelation 12, the twelve tribes of Israel are represented by twelve stars, and the people who will be ruled by Satan (the EU) are also represented by twelve stars. Could this be a coincidence, or maybe a sign?

The anthem of the EU is a hymn Christians sing around the world called "Ode to Joy." Interestingly, the EU has changed the name of the anthem to "Ode to Freedom" (the words have been changed also). Little do the people of the EU realize that in just a short time, their "Ode to Freedom" will be trampled on by their new president, who will demand worship as God and turn Europe into a huge gulag existing only to worship him.

Growth and Setbacks

On January 1, 1995, Jacques Delors's dream of a politically united Europe came one step closer to fulfillment when Sweden, Finland, and Austria joined the EU, bringing the total membership to fifteen. At the time, Norway's ruling party was also seeking membership in the EU, but the voters of that nation rejected membership through a popular referendum. Thus, these three nations would represent the last new members in the EU that Delors would witness as president of the Commission, as his second term in office concluded at the end of 1994.

In 1996, the Intergovernmental Conference was held in Turin, Italy. The objectives of the conference were to reorganize the institutions of the EU to prepare for taking in the Eastern Bloc nations as members and to get ready for the European Monetary Union (EMU). In order to qualify for this union, the nations of the EU had to meet a certain standard of economic and monetary stability. By January 1, 1999, eleven nations of the EU had successfully met these requirements. As some have said, the implementation of this single currency system (the "Euro") marked the true beginning of a united Europe.

Around this time, the EU started to receive criticisms from the rest of the world that there was no one at the wheel and the ship was adrift. The principle objection was that Europe had become an "economic giant but a political pygmy." The question many were asking was, "When I call Europe, who do I ask for?" The two main problems in the development of a political EU at this juncture were the fact that no one individual represented the Union and that the individual member nations were hesitant to give up any part of their national sovereignty.

On November 8, 2000, the Commission reported on the progress of the ten Eastern Bloc candidate countries towards membership and noted that these nations were fulfilling the requirements for membership. However, another candidate, Turkey, was experiencing some roadblocks due to the issue of human rights abuses. To gain acceptance in the EU, a country must not only have a functioning market economy capable of competition within the EU but also a stable democracy that respects human rights and the rule of law. The Commission ultimately decided that Turkey would have to address this problem before it would be considered for membership in the EU.

It is my conviction that the leadership of the EU does not want Turkey to be a member, and that it will never be admitted to the Union. This is because a nation's voting influence in the EU is based on its population. Turkey is a Muslim nation, and because it would have the largest population of any of the EU members, it would be able to dominate any decision made in the EU parliament. Turkey's non-acceptance into the EU may push the nation into the arms of Islamic Turkish militant leaders, who have been lobbying Turkey's government to turn away from the West and install an Islamic state. If this happens, it is very probable that they will join the Russian invasion of Israel, called the "battle of Armageddon" in Ezekiel 38–39. In fact, many believe that the nation of Beth Togarmah, referred to in Ezekiel 38:6, is modern-day Turkey.

On February 26, 2001, the Treaty of Nice (a rewrite of the Maastricht Treaty) was signed by all fifteen EU member states; however, when a referendum on the treaty was held in Ireland, the public voted against it. Irish Prime Minister Berti Ahearn was able eventually to placate the Irish naysayers, and shortly thereafter, the treaty was ratified by all fifteen member nations. In terms of fulfilling biblical prophecy, it was important that Ireland stay in the EU, because that nation represents one of the original ten horns that entered into the Single Market with "one purpose." Ireland had to be in the EU at political unification, where the ten horns give their power and authority to the Beast.

Meanwhile, Great Britain and Denmark held on to the opt-outs from the Maastricht Treaty given to them earlier. Again, this is important, because even though Great Britain and Denmark were members of the EU before the Single Market went on line December 31, 1992, they are not counted as part of the ten horns because of these opt-outs to the Maastricht Treaty that occurred prior to the beginning of the Single Market.

On January 28, 2002, Euro coins and notes became the legal tender of the then twelve nations participating in the EMU, and circulation of all other currency in these member states ceased as of that date. Three other current members of the EU—Great Britain, Denmark, and Sweden—kept their national currencies. The fact that Great Britain kept the sterling and the pound also has prophetic significance, in that it continues to maintain a political distance from those on the continent.

A New Constitution

In December of 2001, the Council of the EU established a body known as the Convention on the Future of Europe. This convention was mainly concerned with framing a European constitution. An early draft for a constitution was ready for presentation to the EU members at the Thessaloniki Summit held in Greece in June of 2003. This draft of the constitution would become the foundation for the upcoming negotiations for the Future of Europe.

During the summit, measures were also put in place to eliminate the need for traveling summits and for a rotating six-month presidency. The EU presidency would be filled by an appointed individual for a renewable two-and-one-half year term. It was also decided during this time that a Minister of Foreign Affairs would be appointed in conjunction with this new long-term president. However, they did not form a federated government at that time.

On May 1, 2004, Estonia, Latvia, Lithuania, Malta, Poland, Slovakia, Slovenia, Czechnia, Hungary, and Cyprus became members of the EU, bringing the grand total to twenty-five countries and adding more than 100 million people to the Union. These later nations are important to the prophetic picture, because with their membership, there are no longer ten sovereign nations in Western Europe outside of the EU that could develop into another ten-horn confederation of Revelation 17. Now, the only way ten nations in Western Europe could attempt to repeat what happened during the birth of the EU is by their leaving all the benefits of the union and withdrawing from membership. These ten nations would also have to meet all the prerequisites set down in Revelation 17, which have already been met by the original ten nations of the Single Market. These prerequisites are:

1. Ten sovereign nations must come together in some sort of federation.

2. All ten nations must rule individually over this federation for a period of time (i.e. the former six-month rotating presidency in the EU).
3. A man must somehow be a part of this federation at its inception, yet his position must also be outside of the ten nations.
4. The ten nations must have "one purpose" to unify politically, and then give this man their individual power and authority.

As you can see, the chances for this scenario to take place a second time are extremely remote. Of course, ten nations could emerge from around the Mediterranean area, because ancient Rome also ruled in that area. However, except for those nations who already belong to the EU and the nation of Israel, that part of the world is basically Muslim, and will later fight against the Beast/Antichrist in the battle of Armageddon.

On June 18, 2004, the European Council in Brussels finalized the draft of the EU's first constitution, and on October 29, 2004, the twenty-five European heads of state signed the document. Shortly after, in May and June of 2005, the French and the Dutch rejected the constitution by referendum, which threw the entire process of unification into chaos. The EU heads of state then decided to temporarily bypass the appointment of a long-term president and retain the six-month rotating presidency. Javier Solana was appointed for an indefinite period to be the new EU Minister of Foreign Affairs.

The Council of Ministers then decided to have a two-year time of "reflection" to find out what went wrong. Many leaders, such as English Prime Minister Tony Blair, declared the constitution to be dead, while others in the EU began scrambling to put Humpty Dumpty back together again. These Humpty-Dumpty builders softened the idea of a constitution by attempting to call it a "treaty," but the other side still maintained it was a constitution. They claimed that the constitution represented a power grab by Brussels and that the adoption of it would move them one step closer to centralized control of the EU member states.

On January 1, 2007, Germany took over the six-month presidency of the EU, under the leadership of Chancellor Angela Merkel. She immediately made the implementation of the constitution by 2009 one of her top priorities and designated the end of 2007 as the target date for completing the revision of the constitution. The same day Germany took over the EU presidency, Bulgaria and Romania joined the EU, bringing the total membership to twenty-seven countries.

The Lisbon Treaty

After the two-year "time of reflection," the EU heads of state met in Lisbon to consider the objections of the French and the Dutch to the EU constitution. Like the rejected constitution before it, the revised Lisbon Treaty proposed a long-term position for the president, although this presidency was now to be just a "figurehead" to replace the unwieldy six-month rotation system of the member nation's leaders. In its place, the position of Foreign Minister was to have more political clout than that of the president.

Leaders of the twenty-seven nations in the EU signed the revised constitution in December of 2007, in a historic Lisbon Monastery. In an attempt to avoid a British referendum vote on the treaty, the British Labor government was again given key opt-outs on foreign policy, labor rights, taxes, and social security systems. The British government approved the treaty opt-outs, but again rejected the Euro currency.

Ireland rejected the Lisbon Treaty by referendum in June of 2008, just as they had rejected the Nice Treaty several years before. This was a big disappointment to the EU Council of Ministers, because the Council had again passed a resolution mandating that all of the member nations had to approve the treaty for it to go into effect. The Council of Ministers were quick to remind the Irish that they had become a wealthy nation because of the huge amounts of cash given to them by the EU. Nonetheless, in December of 2008, EU leaders agreed to a series of concessions to placate the Irish public into accepting the Lisbon Treaty. These concessions included provisions that the EU would not impose rules on Ireland concerning taxation and "ethical issues" (such as abortion, euthanasia, and gay marriages) and that the EU would not interfere with Ireland's traditional neutrality. On October 2, 2009, the Irish ratified the Lisbon Treaty through a renewed referendum.

In June of 2008, just before the French were to assume the six-month presidency and the Council of Minister's semiannual meeting, both houses of the British Parliament, with the Labour Party in the majority, and Queen Elizabeth II signed the United Kingdom's approval of the treaty. A few years before, Tony Blair's Labour Party had come to power in the United Kingdom on the promise that they would place a referendum before the people on membership in the European Union. Eighty-one percent of the British people had been in favor of this referendum, but now they were being denied their right to do so by the same Labour Party they had voted into power. Of course, this did not sit well with the leaders who represented the majority who wanted a referendum on the treaty, and they fought the decision furiously.

In my opinion, the eighty-one percent will eventually prevail, and Britain will withdraw from the EU. Prime Minister Cameron made a speech in 2013 outlining plans for a national referendum in 2015 on whether to enter a new relationship with Europe, or withdraw altogether. Unfortunately, 2015 will be too late since the EU will have politically unified in 2014.

Britain's withdrawal from the EU is prophetically important, because its withdrawal will be a strong indication that it is the lion beast in Daniel 7.

The slow pace toward political unification through the years has been the fact that the member nations didn't really want to give up their sovereignty. When the EU was forced to bail out the member state of Greece, with Spain and Ireland in the wings waiting their turn for a hand-out, it became evident to all that the Euro would suddenly fail if political unification was not realized in the near future.

Prophecy Fulfilled

It is my conviction that the appointment of Jacques Delors by the Council of Ministers as the first president of a politically unified Europe will fulfill Revelation 17:13.

It makes no difference in terms of the fulfillment of Revelation 17:13 that by the time Delors is appointed to the presidency of a unified Europe more countries than the prophetical ten states had joined the EU. The original ten are still members of the EU. Daniel 7:8

makes a distinction between the ten horns and the later horns: "While I was thinking about the horns, there before me was another horn, a little one, which came up among them, and three of the first horns were uprooted before it." This uprooting of three of the *first* horns, or nations, refers to three nations of the original prophetic ten horns of December 31, 1992. This infers that there are other nations that will join with the ten horns.

Dr. Ryrie, a professor at Dallas Theological Seminary, made the following statement in regard to the beginning of the events in the book of Revelation: " 'The Revelation of Jesus Christ, which God gave him to show to His bond-servants, the things which must shortly take place' (Rev. 1:1). 'Shortly.' This word does not indicate that the events described in this book will necessarily occur soon, but when they do begin to happen they will come to pass swiftly (the same Greek word is translated "speedily" in Luke 18:8)."4

If Dr. Ryrie's interpretation is correct, because Revelation 17:12 has now been fulfilled, and Verse 13 is about to be fulfilled, it shouldn't be long before Delors confirms some kind of security treaty with the nation of Israel, which will begin the last seven years before Christ sets up His Millennial Kingdom on earth (see Dan. 9:24). Once Delors signs the treaty, there will be a period of three-and-one-half years before he becomes Satan incarnate. After that, he will live a supernatural life for 1,260 days. (See chapter 9 for an explanation of Daniel's "seventy weeks" from Daniel 9:24–27.)

Summary

The revival of the Roman Empire, represented by the toes of the statue of Daniel 2 and the horns of Daniel 7 and Revelation 17, has manifested itself as the modern-day confederation of nations called the European Union. Six countries came together in 1957 to sign the Treaty of Rome. This was the birth of the European Economic Community or "Common Market," which laid the foundation for future political union.

In 1973, the United Kingdom, Denmark, and Ireland joined the EEC. Prophecy buffs became convinced that the membership of one more nation would complete the prophesied ten nations, which occurred when Greece became the tenth nation in 1981. But these expectations evaporated in 1986, when Spain and Portugal also joined. What was not seen, however, was that biblical prophecy in fact had been fulfilled, because only ten of these nations had signed on to the "one purpose" of the Maastricht Treaty: "They have *one purpose* and will *give* their power and authority to the beast" (Rev. 17:13). England and Denmark took opt-outs, while still remaining within the Single Market, which left these two nations out of the "one purpose" of the other ten nations.

In 1985, Jacques Delors was appointed president of the Commission. Then June 21–22, 2003, at the Thessaloniki Summit, the EU members agreed to a constitution, to the appointment of a foreign minister, and to change the structure of the presidency from a six-month rotating schedule to a renewable two-and-one-half year term for a single individual. France and the Netherlands rejected the constitution by a referendum vote, which caused the Council of Ministers to use creative means to attempt to push through acceptance of a revised constitution.

The revised constitution was called the Lisbon Treaty. In June 2008, Ireland rejected the treaty by referendum, which delayed acceptance of the constitution until 2010. On October 2, 2009, the Irish were given opt-outs from the treaty, and with these concessions, they were brought back into the treaty. On January 1, 2010 the treaty went into force. However, the treaty didn't bring in political unification. It won't be until 2014 that unification will take place for twenty-six countries, Great Britain is expected to withdraw, and the Beast will be given all the powers of a politically unified Europe thus....

THE APOCALYPSE HAS BEGUN.

CHAPTER 2

THE BEAST OF THE APOCALYPSE

As important as it is for us to know that the Apocalypse has begun, it is equally important to understand what is in store for us now that it has started. The problem we face at this juncture is that there has been a plethora of misunderstandings regarding the events of the Apocalypse. So, I will attempt to blaze a trail through what I believe to be a maze of misunderstandings and confusion regarding the end times, and submit what I think to be a Scriptural interpretation of the Apocalypse. This chapter will begin by sorting through some of the possible misconceptions surrounding the Beast of the Apocalypse.

Defining the Beast

The man popularly known as "the Antichrist," or the man against Christ, is only referred to by this name in First and Second John in the Bible. In reading these two books, one gets the impression that John may be writing about a man called "the Antichrist" or "the spirit of the Antichrist." In Daniel and Revelation, we find references to a man called the "Beast," who appears to be the same man as the "Antichrist" in John's books. However, for the sake of clarity, I have chosen to maintain the identification given in Daniel and Revelation and call this man the Beast. Whenever the word "Beast" is capitalized, it will always refer to this man of lawlessness (see 2 Thess. 2:3).

I'm very cautious in naming Mr. Delors as the Beast, and I may appear to be playing the tired old game of "pin the tail on the Beast." I admit it is a game that has been played too many times in the past, and all those who have played it have been proven wrong to the embarrassment of themselves and the rest of the Christian community. Thus, naming Mr. Delors as the Beast is not something I do lightly, but I feel that I would be remiss if I didn't report that which, I believe, has been substantiated by Scripture. My Scriptural basis for doing so is the fact that Rev. 17:12 has been fulfilled. At the time of the fulfillment there was no one but Delors involved in the EU who, in my opinion, could have met the qualifications of the Beast. However, I want to add that this book is being published in 2013, and we all know Shakespeare was right when he wrote "the best laid plans of mice and men oft go awry." This prediction can't be confirmed positively until the political union of the European Union takes place. This event is scheduled for 2014. At that time a president will be appointed who, I am convinced, will be the Beast of Scripture. The Beast had to have been in a prominent position in the EU to have received the "kingdom" along with the ten horns. And, according to Scripture, he has to be the same man in Rev. 17:13. Thus, Jacques Delors becomes the number one suspect.

Up until the time the "ten kings" give the Beast their "power and authority" they are sovereign nations ruling over this "kingdom" (the EU). Once they fulfill Rev. 17:13 by giving over the political reins to the man Scripture calls the Beast Rev. 17:13 can never take place again.

To this end, I believe it is important to go briefly through each of the events that have transpired within the EU to show how they fulfill the prophecies of Revelation 17:12–13 and show why, I believe, Scripture identifies Mr. Jacques Delors as the Beast. In doing so, I'm aware that some of the following material may be redundant, but I feel that it is necessary to include it for clarity.

The ten horns you saw are ten kings who have not yet received a kingdom, but who for one hour will receive authority as kings along with the beast. They have one purpose and will give their power and authority to the beast.

—Revelation 17:12–13

The ten horns you saw are ten kings ... In the Bible, kings are synonymous with kingdoms. The ten kings, or kingdoms, are France, Germany, Italy, the Netherlands, Belgium, Luxembourg, Greece, Spain, Portugal, and Ireland. These ten kingdoms (along with Great Britain and Denmark, who had opt-outs from certain provisions in the treaty, and do not qualify for being part of the ten) formed the Single Market/ European Union on December 31, 1992. The ten kings/kingdoms thus became the ten horns of Scripture.

Who have not yet received a kingdom ... Although the ten nations were in place as of 1986, when Spain and Portugal joined the European Economic Community, they had "not yet received a kingdom," which we identify as the European Single Market.

But who for one hour ... The word "hour" here refers to a short period of time, which turned out to be from December 31, 1992 (the birth of the Single Market) to 2014, when Jacques Delors will be appointed as the president of this new politically unified federation of European nations.

Receive authority as kings ... The European Single Market had the appearance of any other nation of the world. The difference was that instead of having one ruling government, this "kingdom" was ruled by the ten sovereign nations of the EU who had "one purpose."

Along with the beast. Delors presided over the European Commission as president from 1985 to 1995 and was largely responsible for the formation of the Single Market. In 1992, he was said to be the second most powerful man in Europe, next to German ex-chancellor Helmut Kohl. Based on the strength of his leadership, the position of Commission President was elevated to that of a head of state. Thus, Delors was the only man in a position to receive the Single Market (kingdom) along with the ten nations. He had to be a man standing outside of the ten and not have any political connection to any of them but be close enough to be in a leadership position to receive the kingdom along with the ten.

They have one purpose … All ten nations ratified the Maastricht Treaty before the Single Market was put on line. This treaty defined who the ten nations were and served as the foundation for a centralized government. As we mentioned, England and Denmark were Single Market members during this time but took opt-outs from the treaty, which isolated them from having the "one purpose" of the other ten nations.

And will give their power and authority to the beast. According to this prophecy, these sovereign nations must *give* the Beast their power and authority. The fact that the nations in the EU were sovereign *before* the Council of Ministers appoints Delors as its president points to his being the Beast of Revelation 17:12–13. The Beast must be the *first* individual to whom these nations give their power—not the second or third—because after that, they would no longer be sovereign. The nations in the EU will never be sovereign again after this happens, because they will belong to one federal government under the authority of President Delors. According to Scripture, he will be the first and last president of the EU.

Some Common Objections

Some may argue that the man identified as the Beast in Revelation 17:12 is not the same as the Beast in verse 13. However, we know from Scripture that there are only two men called "beasts." The first is the beast from the Sea of Gentile Humanity (see Rev. 13:1). The second beast is the False Prophet, who comes out of the earth (see Rev. 13:11). We know from the context of Revelation 17:12–13 that the man called "the Beast" in these verses is the one from the Sea of Gentile Humanity and not the False Prophet, because the Beast enters the world scene before the seven-year period starts and the False Prophet does not enter until the middle of the seven years.

Some may also argue that Delors could not be the Beast because more than twenty nations in the EU have given their authority to him instead of the ten nations as Scripture states. This is true, but it is important to remember that the original ten nations are within that number. It does not make any difference as to how many nations were in the EU at the time of Delors's appointment. The important point is that the original ten nations, which were present when the Single Market began on December 31, 1992, were members of the EU when they all give Delors their power and authority.

The mindset of many prophecy buffs has been that only ten nations would form this biblical alliance and that only ten would remain throughout the events of the Apocalypse. This is because only the ten horns seem to be mentioned in Scripture. However, by looking closely at Daniel 7:8, we see that the Beast uproots three of the *first* horns, which implies that other horns, or nations, have joined themselves to the original ten.

There is another objection to Delors being the Beast. Being in his 9th decade, many will say that Delors is too old to be the Beast of Scripture. This is most likely due to a popular misconception that Satan will attempt to present the Beast as a young Jewish Messiah, thereby matching the biblical requirements and characteristics of Jesus. Obviously, a parallel in age does not exist between Jesus and Delors. However, the truth is that Delors's age is not relevant. The Bible never states that the Beast will come on the scene claiming to be the Messiah, or the Christ. Daniel 9:27 simply states that the Beast will make a covenant with the nation of Israel for seven years, and that during the middle of these seven years he will set himself up in the Temple at Jerusalem and claim to be God (see 2 Thess. 2:4).

Delors is the only one qualified to fulfill the prophecy of Revelation 17:12–13, because he is the only one who has and is able to meet all of the requirements set down by Scripture:

1. He must be on the scene in a leadership position with the ten nations, but not part of them.
2. He must receive this kingdom along with the ten nations.
3. He must be appointed, not elected, by the ten nations as their first president.
4. He must be the same man who is appointed in Revelation 17:13 as the man who received the kingdom along with the ten nations in verse 12.

As said before, Jacques Delors has met all of these requirements and can thus, I believe, be identified as the Beast of the Apocalypse.

Rise to Power

Many have expected the Beast to step on the world stage as a powerful personality. However, Delors's entrance onto the world stage in 1985, when he became president of the Commission, was made in almost complete obscurity. Even now, his entrance as the Beast has gone almost completely unnoticed. In fact, few people in America have ever heard of Monsieur Jacques Lucien Jean Delors.

During the 1940s and through the 1960s, Delors held a series of posts in French banking and state planning. In 1969, he became an adviser to the Gaullist Prime Minister Jacques Chaban-Delmas. In 1974, he joined the French Socialist Party, and then served in the European Parliament from 1979 to 1981. The knowledge he gained in this position gave him a jump start when he was appointed president of the Commission in 1985. It appeared as if he had been given "the golden handshake" and a job that no one else wanted. However, the position turned out to be, as he described it, "an exciting challenge." It wasn't long before he had turned the ailing institution around and started it moving toward its objective of a single market and eventual political union.

In February of 1989, Delors, already known as "Mr. Europe" in the European press, was featured on the cover of *Newsweek* as the "Czar of Brussels." At one point, Margaret Thatcher branded him "the Beast of Brussels," for she was sure that all Delors wanted was power. What a prophetic statement! Helmut Kohl of Germany respected Delors immensely, and just before Kohl left office, he suggested that Delors be appointed the first president of a unified Europe. Kohl's suggestion years ago may play a part in the presidential appointment of Delors.

Another reason for his appointment may be the fact that he is a brilliant economist. Delors's prowess in the field of economics was proven during his eight years as president of the EU Commission. When the hard questions of money came before the Commission, he was always able to find a way to satisfy all sides of the issue. With the recent events of the world economies going into a tailspin, the EU may have figured that Delors was their best bet to get the EU back on course.

Personal Characteristics

In 1991, John Ardagh wrote the following in the *New York Times* about Delors's abilities to be a mover and shaker in the EU:

> Delors is a civil servant, not an elected politician. As president of the European Commission—the executive and policy planning wing of the European Community—he presided over 16 fellow commissioners and some 10,000 other Euro-staff, but he answers to the 12 heads of state who appointed him. "They are my masters," he says. Yet Delors is treated as their equal; often, in a personal *tour de force* he imposes his will on them.[1]

Delors's main redeeming qualities seem to be the fact that he is a workaholic, has an inexhaustible supply of new ideas, and has a bulldog's tenacity to reach his goals. Charles Grant, in his 1994 biography *Delors: Inside the House that Jacques Built,* remarks that "Delors is a natural dreamer, thinker, strategist and negotiator who prefers to leave bureaucracy—and dirty work—to others."[2] He adds, "At many points in his career, Delors has faced a choice, to hold power, but accept limits on what he may say; or to renounce power, but gain the right to speak freely. Delors has usually chosen power rather than political purity. To Delorists, this is proof of his desire to serve humanity through practical action. To the anti-Delorists, he is a master opportunist."[3]

Delors is said to have an incredible ability to persuade people to his way of thinking. This persuasive style came through in 1988, when he spoke to an unfriendly group at the annual congress of Britain's trade union leaders. Until Delors made this speech, the Labour Party had been adamantly against the idea of having open borders for trade, labor, transportation, and people. Delors, speaking to the crowd in English, presented the idea of a new, prosperous Europe in which workers would benefit more from their labor. When he finished, he received a standing ovation. David Lea, the Deputy Head of Trades Union Congress (Britain's equivalent of the A.F.L.-C.I.O.), made the following remarks about Delors's speech: "It was amazing ... he mirrored all our social ideals and managed to convince us that maybe we could obtain through Europe the things we were blocked by Thatcher here in Britain. He's won over much of the Labour Party, too. He's the kind of European leader of stature we'd been longing for."[4]

Despite these positive traits, Delors appears to be a difficult person to work for. Those who were close to him at the Commission remarked that he had a bristling, unyielding personality and often went through periods of depression. He was emotional, easily hurt, and had a tendency toward occasional tantrums. When things were going well, he was on top of the world; but when things were going against him, he easily became depressed. He had times when he bounced between being arrogant and domineering and being genuinely humble. He would not tolerate imperfection, regardless of whether that imperfection came from his own work or from that of his colleagues. A close friend of Delors once noted that "he lives on his nerves so if something goes wrong he explodes."[5]

In appearance, Delors is short in stature and always impeccably dressed. Most of the time he is reserved, even a little austere, yet he has a commanding presence and an easy-to-listen-to voice. He speaks with a precision and brevity that can seem cutting and abrupt, doesn't smile much, and has little time for small talk. As Grant notes, "Although Delors wears the smartest suits, his stocky build, stiff gait and erect posture gave him a faintly Napoleonic appearance."[6] He attends mass every Sunday, knows the French archbishops, and takes a close interest in the affairs of the Catholic Church. However, he considers himself to be a "secular Catholic" and firmly believes that the Church should stay out of politics.[7]

Those who have known Delors over the years provide some additional insights into his personality. Pierre Mialet, a mathematician, inventor, and sometime president of the French company Camping Gaz, remarked that "Delors had a kind of mysterious radiance: it was hard to classify where he came from or where he was going."[8] Michel Rocard, the leader of the French Socialist opposition, noted that Delores was "a producer of ideas—one is never very sure if he is really in politics."[9] Peter Sutherland, an Irishman in charge of business competition for the EU from 1985 to 1988, remarked that he "liked Delors above all for his intellect: he had the most formidable brain that I have ever encountered. But he was extremely tense, like a coiled spring."[10] Nils Ersboll, the secretary-general of the Council of Ministers, said that Delors was "brilliant at satisfying a country by finding tiny changes in a text, or sum of money, which others would not have thought of because they would not have known the details."[11] And Carlos Westendorp, Spain's minister for Europe, remarks that "Delors has a sense of power and how to exercise it: he uses all possible means to pursue a goal."[12]

In many ways, Delors displays many of the characteristics of a successful political leader. As Grant concludes, "He is a strategist who plots a course and sticks to it with tenacity. He can squeeze a compromise from a group of diverse individuals. He can master a brief and argue a convincing case on television. He knows how to win the attention of journalists and to flatter them. Having held office for so long, he has learned to wield authority and to make subordinates jump. He often has a general's tactical instinct spotting an opening, timing an offensive and concentrating resources on a target."[13]

It is interesting to note that many of these character traits may be expanded and exploited by Satan during the middle of the seven years.

Summary

It is my belief that Scripture and historical events have shown that Mr. Delors is the Beast of the Apocalypse. I believe that this is the case because Delors is the only person who was in the right place at the right time to fulfill the biblical prophecy (to receive the Single Market along with the ten nations). He is completely innocent of any scheme to become the Beast; he is just an ambitious politician with a brilliant mind.

Delors will be the first and last president of the EU, because the ten nations will give their power to (Delors) the Beast, and the Beast is the only president the EU will ever have, as there will no longer be ten sovereign nations to make up another confederation at a future date. Plus, Scripture says the Beast will rule until Christ captures him at Armageddon.

That there are more than ten nations currently in the EU is irrelevant, as the original ten nations that were present when the Single Market began on December 31, 1992 will be present when all the member nations of the EU will give Delors their power and authority.

Delors's advanced age is not relevant to his identification as the Beast, because the Bible does not imply that Satan will attempt to present the Beast as a young Jewish Messiah, as some prophecy buffs have claimed. Prophecy only states that the Beast will make a covenant with the nation of Israel for seven years and at the middle of those seven years he will claim to be God.

Even though the identity of the Beast will be confirmed by his appointment as Europe's first president of a politically unified Europe (the fulfillment of Revelation 17:13), there are still many strange ideas surrounding the biblical man called the "Beast." We will focus on some of these ideas in the next chapter.

CHAPTER 3

THE DUAL ORIGINS OF THE BEAST

In Revelation 13:1–2, John describes the following scene regarding the Beast:

> I saw a beast coming out of the sea. He had ten horns and seven heads, with ten crowns on his horns, and on each head a blasphemous name. The beast I saw resembled a leopard, but had feet like those of a bear and a mouth like that of a lion. The dragon gave the beast his power and his throne and great authority.

In this passage, the Beast is seen coming out of the sea, which most scholars agree refers to the great mass of Gentile Humanity. From this, we know that the Beast will not be a Jew but a Gentile, as he comes out of this Sea of Gentile Humanity.

As we mentioned in the previous chapter, a few Bible scholars insist that the Beast will be of Jewish descent, and will come on the scene pretending to be the Jewish Messiah. They base this claim on John 5:43, where Jesus says, "I have come in my Father's name, and you do not accept me; if someone else comes in his own name, you will accept him." However, they miss the point that Jesus is trying to make to His audience. In this passage, He is speaking hypothetically. He is saying that if someone should come in his own name they would rather accept him than Jesus, who came in the authority of His Father's name. Again, the Beast is not of Jewish descent and does not come on the scene claiming to be the Jewish Messiah. Also, the Beast will not be the Islamic 12th Iman, because he comes "up among" the ten European nations, not out of a well in the Middle East as the Muslim world declares (Dan. 7:8).

In Revelation 17:3–6, we see a depiction of the harlot Church riding on the back of Satan. From this, I believe it is a fair assumption that Delors, coming out of the Gentile world population, will be crowned "Emperor of the Holy Roman Empire" by the Pope some time between now and the last half of the seven years. This crowning would represent an attempt by the Roman Church to regain the prestige and power of the Church's former days of glory. After becoming Emperor, Delors will reinstall the imperial form of government, in which the Emperor of Rome was *both* the government, and also, was worshiped as God. At that time, Delors (incarnate by Satan) will destroy the prostitute Church that has been riding on his back and will invade Israel (see Dan. 11:41). Delors will then enter the Temple at Jerusalem and claim to be God (see 2 Thess. 2:4).

The Beast will be revealed to the Jews at this time as the "man of lawlessness" (see 2 Thess. 2:4). At this point, they will recognize that he is no longer their protector but their destroyer. They will also realize that the seven-year covenant of peace they have made with the Beast is, in reality, a "covenant with death" (see Isa. 28:15).

The Reverse Order of the Beasts

In Revelation 13:2, we see that the Beast, symbolically, has the body of a leopard, the feet of a bear, and the mouth of a lion. These three beasts (leopard, bear, and lion) are also featured in Daniel 7:4–6, but they are presented in *reverse* order to that given in Revelation. Dr. Tim LaHaye, co-founder of the Pre-Trib Research Center and co-author of the bestselling *Left Behind* book series, explains this by stating that Daniel presents the lion first because he is looking forward in time. John is looking back in time, so he presents the lion last.[1]

Most expositors agree with this explanation for the reversal of the beasts. They assume that the lion, the bear, and the leopard of Daniel 7:4–6 represent the ancient empires of Babylon, Medo-Persia, and Greece, respectively. They assign characteristics of each to the empire in which it belongs: Babylon, as a lion, attacked its victims with voracity; the Medo-Persians, as a bear, relentlessly stalked their prey; and the Greeks, as a leopard, swiftly overtook their prey. These expositors then attempt to give the Beast depicted in Revelation 13 the same characteristics as the ones they assigned to the three beasts in Daniel.

I am convinced, however, that the three beasts are presented in reverse order in Revelation 13 because John is depicting a thumbnail sketch of the life of the Beast. Like the leopard of Daniel 7:6, who is given dominion to rule, the Beast is given authority to rule by the ten horns, or ten kings (see Rev. 17:13). This authority to rule represents the first event in the Beast's prophetic career. Like the bear of Daniel 7:5, who holds three ribs (or nations) between its teeth, the Beast uproots three nations of the original ten horns (see Dan. 7:8). Like the lion of Daniel 7:4, who had its kingdom torn away (as represented by its wings being torn off), the Beast will have his kingdom torn away by the Lord Jesus Christ at His return, during the battle of Armageddon.

If we look at the reversal of the beasts in Revelation 13 this way, it not only enables us to view the prophetic life of the Beast in perspective but also allows us to make the connection between the "little horn" of Daniel 7 with the Beast of Revelation 13.

The Heads and the Horns

In Revelation 12:3 and 13:1 we read, "Then another sign appeared in heaven: an enormous red dragon with seven heads and ten horns and seven crowns on his heads…. And I saw a beast coming out of the sea. He had ten horns and seven heads, with ten crowns on his horns and on each head a blasphemous name."

Discovering the meaning of the heads, horns, and crowns is the key to understanding what John is actually saying about the Beast in Revelation 13. The *heads* represent empires; *horns* represent kingdoms, kings, or nations; and *crowns* represent power and authority.

Note in Revelation 12:3 that the seven heads are featured first and have seven crowns, while the ten horns do not have crowns. In Revelation 13:1, the ten horns are featured first and have ten crowns, while the seven heads have no crowns. This reversal of position from one chapter to the next tells us that the power has transferred from the heads to the horns. This infers that the seven heads are empires, not seven emperors of the Roman Empire. This is proven by the fact that the crowns (power and authority) pass from the heads to the ten horns (an empire composed of ten nations) and not to the seventh head.

The seven empires mentioned above are: Egypt, Assyria, Babylon, Medo-Persia, Greece, Rome, and a revival of the Roman Empire. Each of these empires had (or will have) an impact on the nation of Israel. The seventh head represents the ten-horn empire. Notice that this seventh head on the Beast is never seen with a crown on it at the same time as the ten horns. I believe the reason for this is because it would confuse the point being made by Scripture, which is that the heads represent empires.

A Fatal Wound

In Revelation 13:3–4 we read, "One of the heads of the beast seemed to have had a fatal wound, but the fatal wound had been healed. The whole world was astonished and followed the beast. Men worshiped the dragon because he had given authority to the beast, and they also worshiped the beast and asked, 'Who is like the beast? Who can make war against him?'"

Many expositors interpret this to mean that the Beast will be wounded in the head and brought back to life. However, based on our interpretation of the heads, horns, and crowns, we know that the fatal wound has to do with one of the *symbolic* seven heads (empires) and not with the actual head of the man called the Beast. The fact that the seven heads are seven empires eliminates the possibility that the Beast will be fatally wounded in the head and then resurrected.

Notice that Scripture does not say the Beast's *head* (singular) will be wounded unto death. I believe this is done so that the Beast's natural head will not be confused with the symbolic seven heads.

All seven heads, or empires, have been (or will be) persecutors of Israel, and all have passed into history with the exception of the sixth and seventh heads. The sixth head represents ancient Rome, and it is this empire that has received the fatal wound. The old Roman Empire received this death blow when it was invaded by the Visigoths during the late fourth century. However, the sixth head never died but lingered between life and death. Many rulers, such as Adolf Hitler, made futile attempts to resurrect the Roman Empire through conquest. I believe that Scripture states that this seemingly fatal wound on the sixth empire will be healed with the revival of the Roman Empire, which is depicted as the ten horns, or the seventh head.

In Revelation 13:14, John tells us in a straightforward manner that the Beast "was wounded by the sword and yet lived." How can the Beast have this fatal wound and yet live when the Scriptures have already told us that it is an empire that is wounded and yet lived? Since we know that God's Word does not contradict itself, there must be another explanation for the head wound to the Beast.

Over the years, there have been nearly as many interpretations of who this head wound will be inflicted upon as there have been of the number 666. Some have predicted that President Kennedy will rise up from his fatal head wound to become the Beast, while others believe that former rulers, such as Mussolini, Hitler, or even Nero, will rise again from the grave. The list of possibilities goes on and on. However, Scripture says that the Lord Jesus is the resurrection and the life, and only He has the power to give life to those who have gone down to the grave. This, again, is proof that there must be another explanation for the head wound.

If the Scriptures that are related to this question are connected, I believe this enigma becomes understandable. To begin, we must first look back to the imperial form of government that prevailed during the time of the Roman Empire.

Under the imperial form of government, Caesar was personified as the government itself. He autocratically ruled his vast domain. As Roman law and order spread peace to the outer regions of the empire, the people in those areas no longer lived in fear of marauding hordes. They wanted to show their gratitude, while at the same time placating this capricious ruler, so they began to call him a god and worship him. At first, the emperors graciously accepted this worship and used it as a tool to control the masses. But it wasn't long before the Caesars demanded worship from the entire empire. By the time ancient Rome fell, emperor worship was the main tenet of the imperial form of government. So not only was Caesar the personification of the government, but also he was worshiped as a god.

The seventh head (the ten horns) is a revival of the fatally wounded sixth head (the Roman Empire). Thus, when Satan incarnates himself in the Beast during the middle of the seven years, the Beast will install the imperial form of government of ancient Rome over the EU's socialistic democracy. The Beast will now be seen as the personification of both the wounded sixth head and the revived seventh head. The Beast will not be physically wounded and brought back to life; it is only the imperial form of government of ancient Rome, which he personifies, that will be brought back to life. Thus, when we read that the False Prophet will order an image to be set up in honor of the Beast "who is wounded by the sword and yet lived," we know that the Beast is being recognized as the personification of the governments of both the sixth and seventh head. Imperialist Rome will live again as the Beast of the Apocalypse.

Out of the Sea ... Out of the Abyss

In Revelation 13:1–4, we read how the Beast comes out of the sea, which represents the great mass of Gentile Humanity. However, in Revelation 17:3–8, we are given a different description for the origin of the Beast:

> Then the angel carried me away in the Spirit into a desert. There I saw a woman sitting on a scarlet beast that was covered with blasphemous names and had seven heads and ten horns. The woman was dressed in purple and scarlet, and was glittering with gold, precious stones and pearls. She held a golden cup in her hand, filled with abominable things and the filth of her adulteries. This title was written on her forehead:

MYSTERY

BABYLON THE GREAT

THE MOTHER OF PROSTITUTES

AND THE ABOMINATIONS OF THE EARTH.

I saw that the woman was drunk with the blood of the saints, the blood of those who bore testimony to Jesus.

When I saw her, I was greatly astonished. Then the angel said to me: "Why are you astonished? I will explain to you the mystery of the woman and the beast she rides, which has the seven heads and ten horns. The beast, which you saw, once was, now is not, and will come up out of the Abyss and go to his destruction. The inhabitants of the earth whose names have not been written in the book of life from the creation of the world will be astonished when they see the beast, because he once was, now is not, and yet will come.

In this passage, the Beast is said to come out of the Abyss. Is it possible for this man to come from two different locations? Some interpreters have attempted to explain this by stating that this man is "wounded unto death" and then rises up from the grave because he comes from the Abyss. However, Scripture states that the unbelieving dead go to a place called Hades, or Sheol, but never to the Abyss. Therefore, the fact that this man called the Beast comes from the Abyss does not mean that he rises from the dead.

I believe an understanding of Revelation 17:8 can clear up this whole problem of the dual origins of the Beast: "The beast, which you saw, *once was, now is not,* and will come up out of the Abyss and go to his destruction" (italics mine). The Abyss is actually a place of confinement for Satan and his angels until they are thrown into the lake of burning sulfur. In Isaiah 14:12–15, we read how Satan's pride caused him to be thrown out of heaven and cast into the Abyss:

How you have fallen from heaven, O morning star, son of the dawn! You have been cast down to the earth, you who once laid low the nations! You said in your heart, "I will ascend to heaven; I will raise my throne above the stars of God; I will sit enthroned on the mount of assembly, on the utmost heights of the sacred mountain. I will ascend above the tops of the clouds; I will make myself like the Most

High." But you were brought down to the grave, to the depths of the pit.

—Isaiah 14:12–15

"Morning star" is translated "Lucifer" in the Hebrew, which is another name for Satan.

Notice how Lucifer repeatedly says, "I will do this," or "I will do that." He wanted to do his will, not God's. Keeping this in mind, read the following passage from Ezekiel 28:12–17:

> You were the model of perfection, full of wisdom and perfect in beauty. You were in Eden, the garden of God; every precious stone adorned you: ruby, topaz and emerald, chrysolite, onyx and jasper, sapphire, turquoise and beryl. Your settings and mountings were made of gold; on the day you were created they were prepared. You were anointed as a guardian cherub, for so I ordained you. You were on the holy mount of God; you walked among the fiery stones. You were blameless in your ways from the day you were created till wickedness was found in you. Through your widespread trade you were filled with violence, and you sinned. So I drove you in disgrace from the mount of God, and I expelled you, O guardian cherub, from among the fiery stones. Your heart became proud on account of your beauty, and you corrupted your wisdom because of your splendor. So I threw you to the earth; I made a spectacle of you before kings.

These verses were apparently directed to the King of Tyre; however, the King of Tyre was never in the Garden of Eden, so these verses must have a dual application in that they fit the actions of Satan better than the actions of the King of Tyre.

We know from Scripture that Satan was in the Garden of Eden and that he "once was" a guardian cherub who was perfect in beauty and wisdom. But his beauty, wisdom, and power went to his head. He thought he could replace God and stand where God stands, and because of his sin of pride, God removed him. He "now is not" in that high position before God any longer.

To complete this picture of Satan, we are given a description in Revelation 20:1–3; 7–10 of Satan's release from the Abyss and his ultimate judgment in the future:

And I saw an angel coming down out of heaven, having the key to the Abyss and holding in his hand a great chain. He seized the dragon, that ancient serpent, who is the devil, or Satan, and bound him for a thousand years. He threw him into the Abyss, and locked and sealed it over him, to keep him from deceiving the nations anymore until the thousand years were ended. After that, he must be set free for a short time....

When the thousand years are over, Satan will be released from his prison and will go out to deceive the nations in the far corners of the earth—Gog and Magog—to gather them to battle. In number they are like the sand on the seashore. They marched across the breath of the earth and surrounded the camp of God's people, the city he loves. But fire came down from heaven and devoured them. And the devil, who deceived them, was thrown into the lake of burning sulfur, where the beast and the false prophet had been thrown. They will be tormented day and night for ever and ever.

After the Battle of Armageddon, Satan is thrown into the Abyss, and the Beast and the False Prophet are cast into the Lake of Fire. A thousand years later, Satan is released to come up out of the Abyss and deceive the nations again. Those whom he deceives are destroyed by fire from God, and Satan is thrown into the Lake of Fire, where he "goes to his destruction" (Rev. 20:1–10).

From all of this, we can understand that the Beast *does* come from the Sea of Gentile Humanity, but because he will become Satan incarnate in the middle of Daniel's last seven years, it can be said about him (at that time) that he "once was, now is not, and will come up out of the Abyss and go to his destruction." When Satan indwells the Beast in the middle of the seven years, it will no longer be the actions of the Beast that move events along, but the actions of Satan working through the Beast.

The Head "Yet to Come"

In Revelation 17:9–11, we read the following about the Beast "who was, and now is not":

This calls for a mind with wisdom. The seven heads are seven hills on which the woman sits. They are also seven kings. Five have fallen, one is, the other has not yet come; but when he does come he must remain for a little while. The beast who once was, and now is not, is an eighth king. He belongs to the seven and is going to his destruction.

In this passage, we find that the seven heads not only represent seven kingdoms but also represent seven hills (actually mountains, as we will discuss in a later chapter). We have already established that these heads are not men (kings) but empires (kingdoms). The five empires that had fallen by John's time were Egypt, Assyria, Babylon, Medo-Persia, and Greece. Rome was the empire "that is" during the time John wrote. The empire that "has not yet come" is the revival of the Roman Empire in the form of the EU.

The seventh head (which is the same as the ten horns) is represented by the Roman imperial form of government vested in the Beast. This "little while" will extend from the time that Satan becomes incarnate in the Beast, which is from the middle of the seven years (see 2 Thess. 2:2–3), until the time of the battle of Armageddon and Christ's return to earth.

In Revelation 17:11, Satan, who is now incarnate in the Beast, is the one "who once was and now is not," and he is called "an eighth king." Notice that Scripture says he "belongs" to the seven. The Beast/Satan is considered an eighth king because he is the personification of the Roman imperial form of government that was the sixth head, but by installing the imperial form of government over the seventh head he becomes an eighth king.

The bottom line from all these verses we have looked at is that the Beast will not be wounded in the head and then raised from the dead to become the Beast of the Apocalypse. The Beast is a man born like any other man. He will in all probability continue to live a normal life as president of the EU until Satan enters him at the middle of the seven years. When that occurs, the world will be astonished that the Roman Empire again lives, personified in this man who possesses such supernatural authority.

The Mark of the Beast

In the middle of the seven years, Satan, who is now incarnate in the Beast, will attempt to appear as God. The Beast will do signs and wonders as Jesus did, thereby deceiving those who have refused to believe the truth. The False Prophet will direct worship toward the Beast, just like the Holy Spirit does to the Son of God.

In Revelation 13:18, we read, "This calls for wisdom. If anyone has insight let him calculate the number of the beast, for it is man's number. His number is 666." When the Beast comes to power, he will require that all those under his authority receive this identifying mark. Many Christians, Jews, and Muslims will go to their death for refusing to accept this mark. Since the rapture will take place sometime after the middle of the seven years, when the Beast's persecution is "cut short" (see Matt. 24:21–31), this indicates that the church will still be on earth during the time the mark of the Beast is required.

For years, people have tried to calculate the meaning behind the number 666. Some believe the meaning can be determined by using the ancient Hebrew practice of *gematria* (taken from the Greek word *geometry*), in which messages were hidden by assigning letters of the alphabet a numerical value. For example, the number 1 would represent *A*, 2 would represent *B*, 3 would represent *C*, and so on. Using this method during the Second World War, someone "calculated" the number 666 to be Benito Mussolini, the Italian dictator. More recently, when someone calculated the number again, it came up as Henry Kissinger.

According to *Webster's New World Dictionary*, to "calculate" means to determine by arithmetic or by reasoning. In the case of Revelation 13:18, reasoning seems to correlate better with the use of the word "wisdom" than mathematical calculation.

In Christian numerology, God's number is seven; man's number is six (man just doesn't measure up to the perfect number seven). Notice that Revelation 13:18 does not say that 666 is *a* man's number, it just says that "it is man's number." Thus, this number 666 may represent a man trying to be God or Satan's unholy trinity. In time, a more accurate meaning may become clear for what this number represents.

Scripture says that all those living within the Beast's domain will be forced to wear the name or the number of the Beast either on their forehead or their right hand. By taking this mark, a person will be swearing allegiance to the Beast and will be allowed to "buy and sell" (Rev. 13:17). However, by taking the mark, a person also automatically buys a one-way ticket to the Lake of Fire, which will be validated by God at the Great White Throne judgment. There will be no going back for that person after he or she receives the mark.

Now, it's not likely that people would want a "666" tattooed on their forehead or right hand. What this "mark" could represent, however, is an electronic identification chip placed under the skin. With such an implanted device, thieves could not steal a person's identity and money, undocumented foreigners could be identified immediately, business transactions could be handled quickly, and the massive piles of paper that stack up because of paper transactions could be eliminated. This technology is with us today, and more than one American company is now promoting this type of product.

It is important to remember that the chip itself does not represent the "mark of the Beast"; rather, is the act of allowing someone to place the name of the Beast or his number on it that would indicate a commitment to worship the Beast as God. This transaction could only be done with the person's consent. I might add that this will only be required within those countries that the Beast rules, not in the whole world. (We will examine this idea that the Beast does not rule the whole world in a later chapter.)

Summary

French socialist Jacques Delors, whom the Scripture calls the Beast, will come to power when the ten nations (within the EU) willingly gave him their power and authority by appointing him as the first president of a politically unified EU (see Rev. 17:13).

The sixth head, which seemed to have a fatal wound, represents the Roman Empire. This wounded head is healed in the seventh head, which is the revived form of the Roman Empire (known today as the EU).

Delors himself will install the Roman imperial form of government during the middle of Daniel's last seven years (see Dan. 9:27). With this installation he assumes the personification of the government. His government will become both the sixth head (the Roman Empire with the fatal wound) and the seventh head (the EU), which will have the same governmental structure as the sixth head. Delors could then be said to have had a fatal wound that was healed.

In the middle of the seven years, President Delors will be indwelt by Satan. At that time, he could be considered to have come from both the Sea of Gentile Humanity and from the Abyss. Before the rapture of the church (which will occur sometime after the middle of the seven years and the persecution is cut short), Delors will require those under his authority to accept the mark of the Beast. This will likely be in the form of a microchip implanted under the skin. To take the mark of the Beast will eliminate any possibility for an individual ever to go to heaven, as it is a sign of allegiance to the Beast. Many Christians, Jews, and Muslims will go to their death for refusing to accept this mark.

CHAPTER 4

PERSECUTION DURING THE APOCALYPSE

In the near future Delors, acting as the first president of a politically unified Europe, will confirm a covenant with the nation of Israel. This event will usher in the beginning of the last seven years of this age (see Dan. 9:27). At the middle of these seven years, he will begin a persecution of all those who refuse to worship him (see Rev. 12:5).

It is my conviction that traditional futurist scholars have misrepresented these last seven years and distorted the events of the Apocalypse. In this chapter, we will examine these distorted events and take a closer look at what may occur during this period of time.

Traditional Futurist Eschatology

Traditional futurist eschatologists believe that the entire seven years will be a time of persecution. They identify the first three and one-half years as "tribulation" and the last three and one-half years as the "Great Tribulation." From there, they branch into three separate schools of thought that are based on where the rapture should be placed during the seven-year period.

The first group, the pretribulationists, believe the rapture will occur at the beginning the seven-year period. The second group, the midtribulationists, believe it will occur at the middle of the seven years. And the third group, the posttribulationists, believe it will occur at the end of the seven-year period. In this chapter, I've chosen to focus on the pretribulation theory as a representation of all three theories, as it represents the most popular of the three. What can be said about pretribulationism applies, for the most part, to the other two theories.

In order to avoid giving the two periods of the seven years what I consider an incorrect nomenclature, I will avoid using the word "tribulation." My reasoning for this designation is that I find no persecution occurring during the first three and one-half years. Instead, I will use the term "seven years" when referring to the entire seven years, and "three and one-half years" when referring to the first half or last half of Daniel's seven-year period. When I refer to what is called the "Great Tribulation" (a portion of the last three and one-half years), I will use the designation "persecution."

An explanation of the day-of-the-Lord wrath may also be helpful at this point. In the Old Testament, the prophets warned of a time when God would execute His wrath against an unrepentant world. This would be a time of darkness, gloom, and judgment for the sins committed both past and present. The length of time of God's wrath could be in the neighborhood of a year or more, and it will include the trumpet and vial judgments in the book of Revelation. It will begin shortly after the persecution has been cut short and will end when Christ sets up His millennial reign.

The day-of-the-Lord wrath is not to be confused with the coming of the Lord. The coming of the Lord will begin at the rapture of the church and extend through the time of God's wrath against the earth. The coming of the Lord will last until Christ sets foot on the Mount of Olives.

I believe Scripture reveals that persecution will not encompass the entire seven-year period but only during a portion of the last three and one-half years. The persecution will actually begin at the middle of the seven years and end at an indefinite time within the last three and one-half years, when it is cut short (see Matt. 24:21–22).

The rapture will take place just after this persecution of the Beast has been cut short.

Construction Error

It is my belief that pretribulationism has a major flaw in its structural foundation. As you may know, if the foundation of a building is even slightly off square, the problem will grow exponentially worse as the structure goes up. The builder must continue to compensate for the error in some way in order to deliver a finished product. The building may give the appearance of being well-built, but on closer inspection you find that the doors don't close, the windows won't open, the corners aren't square, and the floor sags. It isn't long before you realize that you are standing in a house of cards that may suddenly collapse at any moment.

This is the case with the pretribulation theory. Not unlike a building with a flaw in its structural foundation, pretribulationists, in my opinion, have built a system with a foundation that does not square with the Word of God. With all due respect, I believe the men who formed the pretribulation theory have erroneously placed the day-of-the-Lord wrath at the opening of Daniel's last seven years. Matthew 24:29–41 and Revelation 6:12–17 both say that the day-of-the-Lord wrath falls *within* the seven years, not at the beginning. This incorrect placement has forced pretribulationists to interpret other end-times events in ways that fit their faulty foundation. As a result, people have been misled in their beliefs in important doctrines concerning the end times.

There are many reasons why these scholars have passed by the Scriptures that state the day-of-the-Lord wrath will occur within the seven years. A primary reason is that they have interpreted all of the seals of Revelation 6 to be a time of wrath. The late Dr. Henry C. Thiessen, respected theologian, former chairman of the Faculty of the Graduate School at Wheaton College, author of *Systematic Theology,* and an ardent pretribulationist, wrote the following:

> Futurists interpreters of the Revelation generally hold that [chapters] 6–19 of that book deal with the Tribulation period. Now the main

> features of those chapters are the Seals, the Trumpets and the Wrath
> Vials. But each of these is a judgment that emanates from heaven. It
> is God's visiting of wrath upon this sin-cursed world.[1]

This statement is representative of the basic reasoning why pretribulationists place the day-of-the-Lord wrath at the beginning of the seven
years. As you can see from Thiessen's statement, pretribulationism
maintains that the seals, trumpets, and vials (which they believe make
up the seven years) are all judgments "that emanate from heaven."
Pretribulation scholars point to the breaking of the seals by the Lamb
in Revelation 5 as proof that all the seals are the wrath of God. On the
contrary, we see no wrath in the first seal. The breaking of the seals by
the Lamb of God indicates only that He is sovereign and worthy to
reveal His purposes.

To identify the vials and the trumpet judgments that take place
during the last half of the seven years as part of the persecution is, in
my opinion, misplaced. According to Matthew 24:29, the wrath of
God does not start until after the persecution has ceased. "Immediately
after the distress of those days" (the persecution of the Beast), cosmic
disturbances will occur, and then the wrath of God will fall.

Another problem with the pretribulation theory is that it requires
the rapture to be placed at the opening of Daniel's last seven years
instead of just before the day-of-the-Lord wrath sometime after the
middle of the seven years as Scripture dictates. One way pretribulationists attempt to justify this placement is by claiming that because the
last seven years are part of the sixty-nine sevens (which is a punishment
on the nation of Israel—see Dan. 9:24–27), then the last seven-year
period must also be a time of punishment and wrath. However, by
the expositors connecting the concept of wrath to the word punishment, they make out the Scripture to mean something that was never
intended.

God punished Israel by casting the nation out of the Promised Land
and scattering its inhabitants among the nations. This punishment of the
Jews will continue right up until the end of the seven years. However, it
is unwarranted to identify the entire 490-year period as a time of God's
wrath. According to Scripture, only a short period of time during the last
three and one-half years can be actually considered the wrath of God.

The Seals

As mentioned above, many pretribulationists believe that the seals are included in the wrath of God. Let's take a closer look at this idea. In Revelation 6, we find that the first four seals have to do with the impact of the Beast:

> I watched as the Lamb opened the first of the seven seals. Then I heard one of the four living creatures say in a voice like thunder, "Come!" I looked, and there before me was a white horse! Its rider held a bow, and he was given a crown, and he rode out as a conqueror bent on conquest.
>
> When the Lamb opened the second seal, I heard the second living creature say, "Come!" Then another horse came out, a fiery red one. Its rider was given power to take peace from the earth and to make men slay each other. To him was given a large sword.
>
> When the Lamb opened the third seal, I heard the third living creature say, "Come!" I looked, and there before me was a black horse! Its rider was holding a pair of scales in his hand....
>
> When the Lamb opened the fourth seal, I heard the voice of the fourth living creature say, "Come!" I looked, and there before me was a pale horse! Its rider was named Death, and Hades was following close behind him. They were given power over a fourth of the earth to kill by sword, famine and plague, and by the wild beasts of the earth.
>
> —Revelation 6:1–5; 7–8

Notice in the above passage that each of the four living creatures calls out a different horse, but not a different rider. I believe the reason for this is because it is the Beast who rides all four horses during the first four seals. The first seal represents the Beast's actions during the first three and one-half years. He wears a crown, denoting that the ten nations have already given him their power and authority (see Rev. 17:13). He rides a white horse, showing him to be a conquering victor. He conquers by diplomacy, as seen by the fact that he has a bow but no arrows—he does not possess a complete weapon.

During the first three and one-half years of peace, there will be a few nations that will not join the EU. These nations will be the objects of the Beast's diplomatic conquests. His strongest weapon at this point may be his threat that if these countries do not join the EU, they will be frozen out economically. During this time, he will also confirm a treaty with Israel through diplomacy, assuring their protection. However, in order to not be a paper tiger, he must have the backing of the Council of Ministers, which commands the military of the twenty-six-nation EU.

Hal Lindsey, evangelist, pretribulationist, radio and TV talk show host, and author of *The Late Great Planet Earth*, breaks ranks with other pretribulationists when he writes the following about the first three and one-half years and the opening of the first and second seals:

> During the first three and one-half years of the Tribulation the Antichrist will bring a pseudo-peace to the world. Everyone will be singing his praises as the greatest leader in all human history. But at the midpoint of the Tribulation the second seal is opened, and according to Ezekiel 38 and Daniel 11, Russia, the rider on the red horse, snatches peace from the earth.[2]

While I do not agree with Lindsey as to whom the rider is on the red horse, we do agree that the first three and one-half years are a time of peace and that the second seal is opened after this period of time. Notice in Revelation 6:3–4 that when the second seal is opened, the rider is given a sword with which to take peace from the earth. This implies that there will be peace on the earth *until* the second seal is broken. The second seal won't be broken until the middle of the seven years, when the Beast breaks the peace covenant by invading the sovereign nation of Israel (see Dan. 9:27; 11:4). Even if Israel becomes a member of the EU, the Beast must still invade Israel in order to enter the Temple and set himself up as God.

The red horse of war appears at the middle of the seven years because it is at this point that the Beast, now indwelt by Satan, will demand worship as God. The Roman Catholic Church will not capitulate to this demand, so to end this power struggle, the Beast will burn Vatican City and Rome. He will then expand his empire by waging war against the European and North African nations who have been in opposition to him (see Dan. 11:40). By invading Israel (see Dan. 11:41), he will break the covenant he confirmed three and one-half years earlier (see Dan. 9:27), enter the Temple at Jerusalem, and then set himself up as Emperor God in the Holy of Holies. This event will "reveal" to the Jews that he is their enemy, the "man of lawlessness" (see 2 Thess. 2:3–4).

The black horse of famine follows the red horse of war, just as famine always follows war. Through the Beast's conquests in war, he will be able to seize control of the food supply over the nations he controls. Revelation 13:17 says that during this time, no one will be able to buy or sell unless they bear the mark of the Beast, which will cause a great famine within those areas under the Beast's control. As we mentioned in the last chapter, many who live under his rule will refuse to take the required mark on their forehead or on their right hand and will be put to death.

The Prophet from Hell

When the fourth seal is opened, Death appears riding the pale horse of persecution, with Hades following close behind him. They are given power over a fourth of the earth to kill by sword, famine, plague, and wild beasts. The time frame of this fourth seal (as well as the third seal) overlaps the second seal. Both Death and Hades are given proper names, which suggests that these are actual individuals and not just designations of a condition or place. In addition, they are active—they are given power over people to do with them as they please—which also supports the idea that these designations refer to actual individuals.

I believe the person identified as "Death" is the Beast and "Hades" is the False Prophet. Notice that Revelation 6:8 simply states that they are given power over a fourth of the earth to kill, but not that they actually do kill a fourth of the earth. I believe that this fourth of the earth represents the geographical area of the Roman Empire as depicted in Nebuchadnezzar's dream of the image in Daniel 2.

The reason the False Prophet (Hades) is not seen riding a horse is because it is the Beast who instigates the events represented by each horse. The color of the horse the Beast rides denotes the nature of the event he will inflict upon the earth, and he is the primary cause of this persecution.

The False Prophet is simply the Beast's minister of evil, and his role is to enforce the worship of the Beast. Between the two of them, they will subject all those within the borders of the Beast's kingdom who refuse to worship the Beast to unheard of terror and death.

According to Revelation 13:11, the origin of the False Prophet is from the earth. Many Bible students maintain that this person will be a Jew, because the Greek word for "earth" (*ge*) can also be translated as "land" (referring to the land of Israel). However, when the writers of Scripture refer to the geographical area of Israel, they always call it the "land of Israel" or the "beautiful land." I believe that in this passage the Holy Spirit has led the translators to translate this word as "earth" for a very definite reason.

In 1 Samuel 28, we read that God allowed Samuel to come up out of the earth to speak to King Saul. Samuel was buried in the land of Israel, but the Scriptures definitely say that he came out of the "earth" or "ground," not out of the land.

Samuel did not rise up out of the exact same place as the False Prophet will in the last days, but Samuel did come out of the earth. Before Jesus' resurrection, Hades (or hell) was divided into two compartments, with a great chasm between that divided the believers from the nonbelievers. At Christ's resurrection, the believers in Hades (including Samuel) were taken with Him to heaven. From that time on, Hades has only been occupied by the non-believing dead.

The False Prophet is said to come out of the earth, and he represents the place of the lost dead. Thus, Revelation 6:8 gives him the proper name of "Hades." He is probably a demon lieutenant who has taken on the body of some man, much as Satan will do with the Beast. The False Prophet certainly is not a resurrected man from Hades, as only God has the power of resurrection.

Cause, Time frame, and Scope of the Persecution

To summarize, the persecution will begin when Michael throws Satan out of heaven and down to earth at the middle of the seven years (see Rev. 12–13) and will be cut short sometime during the last three and one-half years (see Matt. 24:22). When Satan is thrown to the earth, he will then indwell the Beast and start the period known as "the time of Jacob's trouble." This will be the time when the Beast persecutes any under his rule who refuse to worship him by not taking his mark on their right hand or forehead. The persecution will be instigated and maintained by the Beast and the False Prophet and has nothing to do with the wrath of God, natural occurrences, nation rising against nation, or wars and rumors of wars. Only those events caused by the Beast and the False Prophet can be considered within the biblical frame work of the persecution.

On the surface, the people's refusal to worship the Beast can be seen as the cause of the persecution. However, there is an underlying cause operating within the permissive will of God, and that is Satan's attempt to destroy all those "who obey God's commandments and hold to the testimony of Jesus" (Rev. 12:17).

Now the persecution by the Beast may be a part of God's permissive will, but it cannot be considered part of the wrath of God. For example, the murder of six million Jews by Hitler during the Second World War was an act of God's permissive will in fulfillment of the prophecy that stated the Jews would be punished wherever they were scattered in the world (see Lev. 26:36). Likewise, this persecution is not a time of God's judgment or wrath against man but a time of man's wrath against man. It finds its tragic roots in the Garden of Eden, when sin entered the world and man's heart became desperately wicked. (Remember, God is not to blame for the fall of man.)

At an undisclosed time during the last three and one-half years cosmic disturbances will begin to occur immediately after the persecution by the Beast has been cut short. After this, the sign of the Son of Man will be seen in the sky (see Matt. 24:29–30), and the nations of the world will realize their mistake in rejecting Jesus Christ. Suddenly, the rapture will take place, and only then will the wrath of God be poured out on an unrepentant world.

As we stated, the pretribulation thesis maintains that the entire seven years is the wrath of God. However, for this to be correct, the seals (or four horsemen) would have to be the wrath of God. Actually, Scripture shows that the seals are the wrath of man up to the time the persecution is cut short, and the wrath of God falls (Matt. 24:29–44). Consequently, if one carries the pretribulation thesis to a conclusion, it is God rather than man who is to blame for all the wars, murders, and crimes that have ever occurred. This is just what Satan wants us to believe: that God is responsible for sin and that mankind is innocent. This makes man unaccountable for his behavior; and if he is not accountable, he is not a sinner. Therefore, man would have no need of a Savior.

A major problem for pretribulationists is their inability to agree on what constitutes the persecution that they believe will take place during the first half of the seven-year period. Some say that it will be the natural phenomena of earthquakes, famines, or world events such as wars and rumors of wars and nation rising against nation. Others say that the Beast will bring on persecution during the first half of the seven years in the spiritual realm. Under this theory, the Beast will be supernatural during the first half (which, according to Scripture, he is not), and people will be deluded by his supernatural feats. Consequently, spiritual persecution will come to those who believe "the lie" spoken of in 2 Thessalonians 2 and sell their souls to the Beast. Still others believe Daniel's last seven years consist of all the above. All of this confusion comes from the pretribulationists' attempts to maintain a full seven years of persecution.

The geographical scope of the persecution will be limited to Europe and some countries around the Mediterranean Sea. Given this, it would seem that those who are persecuted by the Beast could avoid the persecution by simply emigrating to another country not under his control. However, we know that not many Jews were able to escape from Nazi Germany during the Second World War. And who can forget the prison created by the Iron Curtain of communist Russia? Today, the locations of individuals can be tracked anywhere in the world through Global Positioning Systems, which may be used in conjunction with the mark of the Beast.

The Persecution in Israel

Daniel 9:27 tells us that the Beast will confirm a covenant with the sovereign nation of Israel for seven years. This covenant is thought to be a protective peace covenant, because Israel will be sovereign at the time the treaty is signed. This verse also affirms that the Beast then will break this covenant by invading Israel in the middle of this seven-year period (see Dan. 11:41) and then force his way into the Holy of Holies in the Temple (see Dan. 9:27).

There are those who are convinced that after signing the covenant with Israel, the Beast will turn and begin persecuting those who refuse to take the mark and live outside of Israel, leaving the persecution of the nation of Israel until the middle of the seven years. The advantage of this thesis is that the Beast could begin his persecution at the start of the seven years and not go into the Temple until the middle of the seven years, as 2 Thessalonians 2:4 says he does. This thesis is a complete fabrication and has no basis in Scripture. There is no persecution by the Beast during the first half of the seven years. The Beast is given only the last half of the seven years to exercise his power (see Rev. 12:5). Daniel 9:27 tells us that the Israelis will feel so secure during the first three and one-half years that they will build the Temple on the Temple Mount and:

> He will confirm a covenant with many for one seven. In the middle of the seven he will put an end to sacrifice and offering. And on a wing of the Temple he will set up an abomination that causes desolation, until the end that is decreed is poured out on him.

Certainly, if the Beast were to begin his persecution of the Jews during the first three-and-one-half-years period, the first place he would start would be at the Temple. However, Scripture tells us time and again that it is not until the middle of the seven years that he enters the Temple and begins his persecutions (see Dan. 12:7; Rev. 11:2; 13:5). I believe it is safe to assume that Jews and Christians living throughout the Beast's empire at that time will also be enjoying the same kind of freedom.

The Sovereignty of Israel

A friend of mine who lived in communist Hungary told me that "peace was everywhere behind the iron curtain, but many at the same time were suffering in the Russian gulags." Based on his experience, my friend believes that both peace and persecution will exist after the covenant is confirmed during the first half of the seven years. However, it is important to remember that the situation in Hungary was very different in comparison to what will take place during the first three and one-half years in Israel. Hungary was not sovereign under Russian domination, whereas Israel will be sovereign before and during the first three and one-half years of the treaty.

It is probable that the EU will pressure the sovereign nation of Israel to accept a seven-year treaty. The conditions of the treaty will most likely be similar to ones Israel has experienced in the past: land for a Palestinian state in return for a guarantee of seven years of peace. The land that Israel gives up may be more than is currently being demanded by the Palestinian Liberation Organization, but in exchange, Israel will be allowed to build on the Temple Mount.

For the Muslims, giving up the Temple Mount—a place where the Jews are currently forbidden even to pray—will represent a major concession to the rest of the world. However, Muslims will go along with the peace treaty because they will gain Israeli land without having to fire a shot, and they will look on the treaty as "not worth the paper it is written on." It has been said by many of Israel's observers that the world of Islam will never be satisfied until they have pushed Israel into the sea.

Another scenario for the treaty may be that Israel will be invited to join the EU, then the EU would be responsible for the safety of Israel. If the EU was able to bring peace to the Middle East, it would gain a tremendous amount of prestige around the world. It would be a slap in the face for the Americans, who have failed after trying so hard to negotiate peace in that area of the world. Somehow, the Beast will be able to maintain the peace for the first three and one-half years. After that time he invades Israel and sets himself up as "God" in the Temple.

In regard to the idea of the Beast's control over Israel, note that there would be no reason for the Beast to make a treaty with Israel if it wasn't sovereign at the time of the treaty. A sovereign nation would not overtly allow another nation to persecute its people while maintaining its sovereignty. Revelation 11:2, which discusses the Temple to be built during the last seven years, supports this idea: "But exclude the outer court; do not measure it, because it has been given to the Gentiles.

They will trample on the holy city for 42 months." The Gentiles will overrun Jerusalem only during the *last half* of the seven years, not the entire seven years. Israel will be sovereign for forty-two months of the seven years, which is one of the reasons the Beast will not dominate it or persecute its people during that time.

Revelation 13:5 states that the Beast will be allowed only forty-two months to exercise his authority. Nowhere in Scripture is the Beast given eighty-four months or seven years to exercise his authority. It is only after he becomes supernatural at the middle of the seven years that he will begin to believe that he is God and starts his persecutions of all those who refuse to worship him. However, as we discussed, even though the Beast is given forty-two months (the second half of the seven years) to exercise his authority, his persecution of those without the mark will be cut short before the end of the seven years.

Signs of the End of the Age

In Matthew 24:2, as Jesus is leaving the Temple in Jerusalem, he tells His disciples that "not one stone [of the Temple] will be left on another; every one will be thrown down." Later, this prompts the disciples to ask what will be the sign of His return and the end of the age. Jesus responds as follows:

> Watch out that no one deceives you. For many will come in my name, claiming, "I am the Christ," and will deceive many. You will hear of wars and rumors of wars, but see to it that you are not alarmed. Such things must happen, but the end is still to come. Nation will rise against nation and kingdom against kingdom. There will be famines and earthquakes in various places. All these are the beginning of birth pains.
>
> Then you will be handed over to be persecuted and put to death, and you will be hated by all nations because of me. At that time many will turn away from the faith and will betray and hate each other, and many false prophets will appear and deceive many people. Because of the increase of wickedness, the love of most will grow cold, but he who stands firm to the end will be saved. And this gospel of the kingdom will be preached in the whole world as a testimony to all nations, and then the end will come.

So when you see standing in the holy place "the abomination that causes desolation" spoken of through the prophet Daniel—let the reader understand—then let those who are in Judah flee to the mountains. Let no one on the top of his house go down to take anything out of the house. Let no one in the field go back to get his cloak. How dreadful it will be in those days for pregnant women and nursing mothers! Pray that your flight will not take place in winter or on the Sabbath. For there will be great distress, unequaled from the beginning of the world until now—and never to be equaled again. If those days had not been cut short, no one would survive, but for the sake of the elect those days will be shortened. At that time if anyone says to you, "Look, here is the Christ!" or, "There he is!" do not believe it. For false Christs and false prophets will appear and perform great signs and miracles to deceive even the elect—if that were possible. See I have told you ahead of time.

So if anyone tells you, "There he is, out in the desert," do not go out; or, "Here he is in the inner room," do not believe it.

—Matt. 24:4–26

Many pretribulationists conclude that the events in Matthew 24:4–8 represent the first half of seven years of supposed persecution (some expositors also include verse 9, while others even include verse 14). They do this even though Scripture gives no indication of persecution during the first half of the seven-year period. As Marvin J. Rosenthal, noted author, lecturer, CEO of Zion's Hope, and editor of *Zion's Fire* states:

The term tribulation period is normally used by pretribulation rapturists as a synonym for the seventieth week of Daniel (Dan. 9:27); that is, to describe the seven years that immediately precede Christ's physical return to the earth to establish His millennial kingdom. Although popular and used by competent preachers, teachers, and theologians, such a designation has no Biblical justification.... A clear fact emerges from an examination of the word tribulation as used in the Bible. In a prophetic context, it is used to describe the period of time that begins in the middle of Daniel's seventieth week—never to the first half of it. Based on that indisputable fact, to call the entire seven year time frame the tribulation period is to coin a technical phrase and superimpose it upon the Scriptures, reading into the Biblical text that which it does not itself declare.[3]

In rebuttal to Rosenthal's statement, Dr. John McLean, a Christian academic and pretribulationist, wrote the following:

> Rosenthal has not only overstated his case but has stated as true fact that which is clearly false. A cursory reading of a Greek concordance reveals that the word "tribulation" is used in prophetic context to refer to both the first and second halves of the seventieth week of Daniel. Matthew 24:9, which chronologically relates to the first half of the seventieth week as evidenced by its preceding the midpoint of the abomination of desolation, (Matt. 24:15–21), states: "Then they will deliver you to tribulation, and will kill you, and you will be hated by all nations on account of my name." Clearly the Biblical text describes the first half of the seventieth week as a time of tribulation.[4]

In this quote, McLean makes three assumptions. First, he asserts that the events of Matthew 24:4–15 are chronological, which, in my opinion, is not the case. Second, he envisions that Jesus' discussion encompasses the complete seven years in Matthew 24, but Scripture indicates that Jesus is only referring to the last three and one-half years beginning at verse 9. Third, he believes that the events from verse 4 to verse 15 (the abomination of desolation) happen during the first half of the seven-year period. He fails to see the connection verse 9 has to verse 15 and that the events depicted in both verses take place during the last three and one-half years.

McLean's position is only one of four theories that attempt to reconcile the entire seven years as a period of persecution (tribulation) within the text of Matthew 24. These four theories are:

1. *The events of Matthew 24:4–8 occur prior to the beginning of Daniel's last seven years and take place during the Church Age.* The events listed in Matthew 24 prior to verse 9 (i.e., false christs, wars, famines, nation rising against nation, earthquakes) have occurred in the last fifty years; thus the events depicted in verse 9 must start the seven years of persecution. The middle of the seven years would then start with verse 15, when the Antichrist sets up the "abomination that causes desolation."

2. *The events of Matthew 24:4–14 have multiple interpretations.* The events in these verses occur both in the Church Age and during the seven-year period.

3. *Only the events of Matthew 24:4–8 occur within the first half of the seven years.* The events in verses 9 to 26 would then occur in the last half of the seven years.

4. *Only the events of Matthew 24:4–14 occur within the first half of the seven years.* The events in verses 15 to 26 would then occur in the last half of the seven years.

I believe that there is one other possibility: the "birth pains" described in Matthew 24:4–8 began in 1948 with the birth of the nation Israel. From that time to the middle of the seven years, we will see false christs, wars, rumors of wars, nation rising against nation, famines, and earthquakes. These "birth pains," which will increase in intensity, are indicators of the coming persecution, which will start in the middle of the seven years (Matt. 24:9).

Even though the entire seven years are "decreed" on the Jews (see Dan. 9:24), Jesus does not dwell on the first three and one-half years in Matthew 24 because the Jews are not being persecuted during that time. In fact, there is no persecution caused by the Beast anywhere in the world at that time. Jesus' focus is on the last half of the seven years, during the "time of Jacob's trouble," when the Beast will impact the Jewish nation. The first eight verses of Matthew 24 are an explanation of what to look for as the time of Jacob's trouble approaches. The last half of the seven years is seen in verses 9 to 29.

Notice the wording in these verses. The "then" at the beginning of verse 9 signals a transition from verses 4 to 8. In other words, the Jews will be persecuted and killed after the events of verses 4 to 8 have taken place. The "so when" of verse 15 relates to the events of verse 9: the abomination of desolation. We know from Daniel 9:27 that the events of the abomination of desolation will take place at the middle of the seven years. Thus, in verses 9 to 13, Jesus is saying that the persecutions will begin at the last three and one-half years—when the Beast enters the Temple, sets up his abomination that causes desolation, and kills all those who refuse to worship his image.

In verse 14, Jesus tells the disciples that the gospel of the kingdom must be preached to the whole world as a testimony before the end of the age. In verse 15, He tells them *when* the persecution is going to happen, and then in verses 16 to 21, He tells them *what to do when it happens.*

The Aorist Tense

Returning to the description of the seals in Revelation 6, pretribulationists divide the seven years by placing the first five seals within the first half of the seven years and the sixth seal, where Scripture states that those hiding in caves call out to the mountains and rocks to "fall on us and hide us from the face of him who sits on the throne and from the wrath of the Lamb! For the great day of their wrath has come, and who can stand?" (Rev. 6:16-17), within the last half of the seven years. To maintain their assertion that the wrath of God takes place at the *beginning* of the seven years, they state that John was writing this passage in what is known as the "aorist tense."

One of the uses of the Greek aorist tense is to refer to a past action. Pretribulationists apply this to Revelation 6:17 and interpret the words "has come" in the past tense, indicating that the wrath of God has already started sometime before the events of this verse. However, Alan Kurschner, M.A., Ph.D. in ancient languages from Gordon Conwell Theological Seminary, notes the following about the use of the aorist tense:

> The aorist does not denote "past time" as some commonly understand it; and it does not denote a "once-for-all action." Some wrongly believe that it is a past tense because it can often be in a past action context. Though it is commonly in past action, it can also be an action in the present, future, or just timeless. Only context—not the fact it is aorist—tells us what time the action occurs. The aorist is what is called the "indefinite" or "undefined" tense. It does not tell you the type of action such as specifying its duration, nor again does it tell the time that the action takes place. The aorist tense is often known as the "background," "snapshot" or "summary" tense (there are some nuances to those notions). Sometimes, it is thought of as the "default" tense in Greek, though that might be too much of an understatement of its function. An author would choose the

aorist tense to represent the action of the verb as a complete whole, i.e. stating an undefined action without giving specific information of the type of action such as focusing on the beginning or ending of the action, its duration, or whether it is repeated or not. That information about the action of the verb can only come through lexical, grammatical or other contextual indicators, and not its tense.

Using contextual indicators in Revelation 6:17 for the aorist tense of "has come" places it in the present tense and definitely not in the past tense. Notice that the cosmic disturbances in Revelation 6:12–14 occur just before the announcement in verses 16 to 17 that the wrath has come. This is the same sequence of events as in Matthew 24:29–41: the cosmic disturbances come first, and the wrath of God follows. To argue otherwise is an attempt to force the Scriptures into the pretribulation scenario. Thus, while it is true that the seven seals may represent the entire seven-year period of Daniel's seventieth seven, they *do not* represent seven years of persecution.

A Bridge to Nowhere

Many futurist interpreters attempt to forge a parallel bridge between the events of Matthew 24:4–14 and the seals of Revelation 6. By stating that the events depicted in the two passages can be seen in parallel *and* in chronological order, they open the door for making the case that Jesus is speaking of seven years of persecution in Matthew 24.

In order to show that no such bridge exists, I've made a comparison between the two passages of Scripture in question. Note that not all the seals will be compared, as it is given that the events of the last three and one-half years appear in both chapters. At the conclusion of this analysis, if we find that just one event in the two passages of Scripture is not parallel and does not appear in chronological order, we must conclude that the pretribulationists have chosen an incorrect interpretation.

Matthew 24:5	Revelation 6:1–2
False Christs	The first seal: the Beast enters

There is no real parallel here, because the Beast never claims to be the Christ at any time. When he demands worship during the middle of the seven years, he does so as Emperor God, not as Jehovah God or the Messiah, as many have assumed.

An argument may be made that the Jews will see the Beast as a conquering deliverer at the time he confirms the covenant to protect the nation of Israel (this will occur at the beginning of the seven years; see Dan. 9:27). However, the "conquering deliverer" designation for the Beast is not likely, because it is generally accepted that the main purpose of the covenant will be to force a Palestinian state within the present borders of Israel. As we discussed, Israel's compensation will be a guarantee of protection for seven years and the ability to erect the Temple on the Temple Mount. When the Israelis are forced to give up land for peace, there will be many Jews who will not think kindly about the covenant or its guarantor.

In addition, because the Beast is not a Jew, he cannot be the conquering deliverer whom many Jews envision today. Remember that Revelation 13:1 says he comes "out of the sea," and that this "sea" represents the Gentile population of the world. The Jews would never accept a Gentile as their conquering deliverer, nor as their Messiah. (In any event, this is a moot point now that Jacques Delors has been identified as the Beast.)

Matthew 24:6–7	Revelation 6:3–4
Wars and rumors of wars	The second seal: war

This is a parallel event with a problem. It is in sequence; however, it is not in chronological order. Revelation 6:3–4, the second seal, refers to a singular war waged by the Beast that takes place during the last half of the seven years. In Matthew 24:6–7, the wars are plural and are connected to the statement of nation rising against nation and kingdom against kingdom. Chronologically, there is no connection between the wars of Matthew 24:6–7 and the war of the rider on the red horse in Revelation 6:3.

Matthew 24:7	Revelation 6:5–6
Famines	The third seal: famine

This, again, is a parallel event that is not in chronological order. The famine seal opens after the war seal, which takes place during the middle of the seven years, not during the first three and one-half years.

Matthew 24:7	Revelation 6:7–8
Earthquakes	The fourth seal: persecutions

There is no earthquake in the fourth seal, which makes it out of sequence with the events depicted in Matthew 24. In the Matthew passage, the persecutions do not begin until verse 9, which starts the last half of the seven years. Pretribulationists believe verse 9 is in the first half of the seven years.

In the following quote, Dr. J. Dwight Pentecost, a Dallas Seminary professor, pretribulationist, Bible scholar, and author of *Things to Come* does not agree with his fellow pretributionists that Matthew 24:9 is within the first three and one-half years. He states:

There are indications that verses 9–26 [of Matthew 24] describe the events of the last half of the week. The abomination of desolation (24:15) is clearly stated by Daniel (9:27) to appear in the middle of the week and continues to the end of the period. The word "then" in verse 9 seems to introduce the persecutions against Israel that were promised them and were described in Revelation 12:12–17, where John reveals that this persecution will last for the last half of the tribulation period (Rev. 12:14). The Lord's outline of the events of the tribulation period can thus be determined. In the first half of the week Israel will experience the chastisements of the events of verses 4–8 (the seals of Rev. 6). Although they will dwell in relative safety under the false covenant.[5]

—Daniel 9:27

I couldn't agree more with Dr. Pentecost's assessment of the placement of events in Matthew 24:9 during the last half of the seven years.

Regrettably, in this paragraph he also picks up the pretribulationist argument for a connection between the seals of Revelation 6 and the events of Matthew 24:4–8, which have just been shown to have no connection whatsoever.

With all due respect to Dr. Pentecost, it would not be possible for Israel to "dwell in relative safety" during the first three and one-half years and at the same time "experience the chastisements of the events in verses 4–8 (the seals of Revelation 6)."

As I mentioned, the events of Matthew 24:4–8 serve as a prophetic signpost that the persecution is coming. These events are not unique to the first three and one-half years of the last seven years. They began in 1948 with the rebirth of the nation of Israel. Through the years, we have seen these signs happening. Many have come claiming to be the Christ. The rise of communism was a major cause of nation rising against nation and kingdom against kingdom. Earthquakes and famines have continued to multiply during the last sixty years. Remember, it will be the *actions of the Beast*, when he becomes satanically supernatural in the middle of the seven years, that will cause the persecution.

Because tribulationists base their theory on the premise that there will be seven years of persecution, they continue to misplace end-times events. Hopefully, this will be made very clear in the next chapter when we look at 2 Thessalonians 2 and the timing of the rapture.

Summary

Traditional futurist eschatologists believe that the entire seven years will be a time of persecution, but this forces an unnatural interpretation of Scripture. The persecution will be a time of *man's* (the Beast's) wrath against man, which will take place at the beginning of the last half of the seven years. This persecution is caused by the Beast, not by world happenings such as wars between nations or earthquakes and famines that are spoken of in Matthew 24:4–8. *God's* wrath against man in the day of the Lord will not begin until the persecution has been "cut short" sometime before the end of the seven years.

It is my belief that it is the Beast who rides all four horses during the first four seals. The first seal represents the Beast's actions during the first three and one-half years, while the second seal initiates the events that will occur during the second three and one-half years, when the Beast, now indwelt by Satan, will demand worship as God. The third and fourth seals overlap the second seal in terms of chronology of events.

Daniel 9:27 states that the Beast will confirm a covenant with the sovereign nation of Israel for seven years. It is likely that this indicates that the EU will pressure the sovereign nation of Israel to accept a seven-year treaty in which the Israelis give up land for a Palestinian state in return for a guarantee of seven years of peace and the ability to build the Temple on the Temple Mount, or perhaps Israel will be invited to join the EU. The EU would then be Israel's protector. The first three-and-one-half-year period will be a time of relative peace for both Jews and Christians living throughout the Beast's empire. After that time, the Beast will enter the Temple and begin his persecutions. The Beast will be allowed forty-two months to exercise his authority and persecute those without the mark, but his persecution will be cut short before the end of the seven years. However, his authority given to him from Satan will continue until the end of the seven years.

In Matthew 24:4–26, Jesus related some of the signs of the end of the age to His disciples. Many pretribulation scholars attempt to create a parallel between the events in this passage and the depiction of the events in the seals in Revelation 6. However, clearly no such parallel structure exists. According to pretribulation theory, the events of both Revelation 6 and Matthew 24:4–8 must be *parallel* and in *chronological sequence* in order to qualify for the supposed connecting bridge between the two chapters. The events do not meet these criteria. Therefore, it must be concluded that a seven-year period of persecution is nonexistent in Matthew 24. There will only be a confined period of persecution, beginning at the middle of the seven years, which will stop before the end of the last three and one-half years, leaving time for the wrath of God.

CHAPTER 5

THE RAPTURE OF
THE CHURCH

Someone has said, "Christianity begins where religion ends.... at the Resurrection." Because Christ was resurrected, all who believe in Him will be resurrected at His return. In the blink of an eye, He will raise all committed followers, both living and dead, into the clouds to be with Him for eternity. This event is known as the rapture. With the pages of the book of Revelation unfolding before us, and the events of the Apocalypse running their course, this unprecedented event cannot be far behind. This chapter will attempt to deal with the timing of this glorious event from a pre-wrath rapture perspective.

For those unfamiliar with the rapture, the apostle Paul describes it as follows:

Brothers, we do not want you to be ignorant about those who fall asleep, or grieve like the rest of men, who have no hope. We believe that Jesus died and rose again, and so we believe that God will bring with Jesus those who have fallen asleep in him. According to the

Lord's own word, we tell you that we who are still alive, who are left till the coming of the Lord, will certainly not precede those who have fallen asleep. For the Lord himself will come down from heaven, with a loud command, with the voice of the archangel and with the trumpet call of God, and the dead in Christ will rise first. After that, we who are still alive and are left will be caught up together with them in the clouds to meet the Lord in the air. And so we will be with the Lord forever. Therefore encourage each other with these words.

—1 Thessalonians 4:13–18

Notice in these verses that Paul associates the rapture with the coming of the Lord. This is a crucial point in our discussion about the timing of the rapture. There is only one coming of the Lord, and the rapture is an inseparable part of that coming.

THE PRETRIBULATION RAPTURE

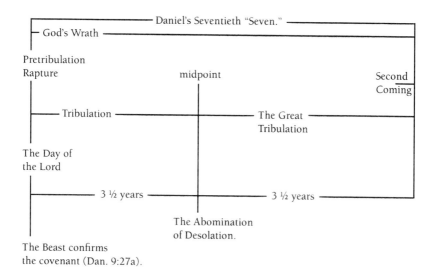

THE PRE-WRATH RAPTURE

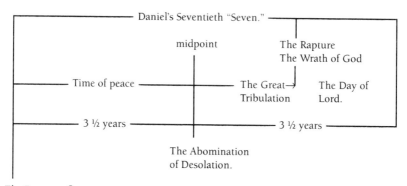

The Pre-Wrath Rapture

The "pre-wrath rapture" concept takes the position that the rapture will take place shortly after the persecution of the Beast has been cut short. Immediately after this event, cosmic disturbances will begin, and the sign of the Son of Man will be seen in the sky. Then the rapture will take place. This occurs on the same day, though slightly before, the day-of-the-Lord wrath falls on an unrepentant world. (The "day of the Lord" and the "wrath of God" will begin on the same day, thus the expression the "day-of-the-Lord wrath.") This is the pre-wrath rapture (see Matt. 24:29–31).

Some may wonder what advantage there is in knowing the timing of the rapture. After all, if we are committed followers of Christ, we are ready to go any time the rapture occurs. While this is true, this line of thinking tends to be self-centered. Hebrews 11:7 says, "By faith Noah, when warned about things not yet seen, in holy fear built an ark to save his family. By faith he condemned the world and became heir of the righteousness that comes by faith." In other words, after Noah was warned of "things not yet seen," he not only acted on God's word to save himself and his family, but he also attempted to reach out to the lost around him. Through his actions, the world stood condemned.

Noah was a witness to the world of God's coming judgment and God's offer of salvation through the ark. Anyone could have joined Noah and his family had they chosen to do so. Entrance into the ark was a step of faith in what God said was going to occur. Sadly, only Noah and his family accepted the message and acted on it; the rest of the world was swept away. The rapture will come about in much the same manner. Every Christian is a present-day Noah. We have been warned through God's Word about "things not yet seen," and we must act as Noah did to warn a lost world of the coming judgment and God's provision of salvation through Jesus. This message must not be distorted, nor should the placement of the rapture during end-times events be based on incorrect data, because it is a matter of life and death.

Also, since the persecution of the Beast starts before the rapture, many might fall away thinking they may have missed the rapture based on the Pretribulation theory.

Sons of Light

In 1 Thessalonians 5:1, Paul writes, "Now, brothers, about times and dates we do not need to write to you?" Since Paul has just finished giving a detailed description of the rapture (see 1 Thess. 4:13–18), we can safely assume that these "times and dates" refer to the rapture and the coming of the Lord. Then Paul writes, "for you know very well that the day of the Lord will come like a thief in the night" (1 Thess. 5:2). Seemingly, prior to writing this letter he had told the Thessalonian church that the rapture would take place on the same day as the day of the Lord and that the day of the Lord would come unexpectedly.

Continuing on, Paul writes, "But you, brothers, are not in darkness so that this day should surprise you like a thief" (1 Thess. 5:4). Paul then assures the Thessalonians that they are sons of light. He states that as the day of the Lord approaches, they will recognize it and not be caught unaware of what is happening.

In Matthew 24:44, Jesus says, "the Son of Man will come at an hour when you do not expect him." I believe this "you" is being used in a generic sense—Jesus is referring to unbelievers who are children of darkness. In Matthew 24:38, He states that it was the unbelievers who didn't see the flood coming until it was too late. Noah did see it coming, for as a believer, God had warned him that the flood would come in 120 years. Noah was only given the general time frame for when the flood would occur, not the exact "day or hour" (see Matt. 25:13). In the same way, believers today have been warned through Scripture as to when the rapture and the wrath of God will take place, but they have not been given the specific day or hour.

In 1 Thessalonians 5:9, Paul says, "For God did not appoint us to suffer wrath but to receive salvation through our Lord Jesus Christ." Paul tells the Christians that they will not go through the wrath of God. However, nowhere in Scripture does it say that Christians will be exempt from the persecution of the Beast.

The Persecution and the Wrath of God

Between the time of the persecution and the day-of-the-Lord wrath, cosmic disturbances will occur. In Joel 2:30–31, the prophet verifies that cosmic disturbances must come before the day of the Lord. These same cosmic disturbances are seen in Revelation 6:12, 14 and again in Matthew 24:29. From this, we can determine that *the wrath of God, but not the persecution of the Beast, falls within the day of the Lord.* We know this separation exists not only because of the fact that the persecution is cut short before the wrath of God falls, but also because of the fact that the cosmic disturbances take place *between* the persecution and the wrath of God.

In Revelation 6:9, when the Lamb opens the fifth seal, we see that God is not yet judging or pouring out His end-times wrath on the world. Instead, the scene depicts those who have been murdered by the Beast during the persecution (which began when the second seal was opened during the middle of the seven years). They call out to the Lord, saying, "How long, Sovereign Lord . . . until you judge the inhabitants of the earth and avenge our blood?" (Rev. 6:10). From this, it is clear that they realize their deaths were caused by the persecution of the Beast and not the wrath of God. They are then given white robes and told to wait "a little longer, until the number of their fellow servants and brothers who were to be killed as they had been was completed" (Rev. 6:11). The completion of these killings will be at the end of the "cut short" persecution, while the vengeance for their deaths will be the wrath of God, which will fall shortly afterward.

The Man of Lawlessness

Sometime after Paul wrote his first letter to the Thessalonians, the believers in the church evidently received a spurious letter stating that they *were already in* the day of the Lord. This was very upsetting to them, because if it were true, it meant they had either missed the rapture or there hadn't been one. Paul responded in his second letter by stressing the connection between the coming of the Lord and the rapture. In 2 Thessalonians 2:1–4, he writes:

> Concerning the coming of our Lord Jesus Christ and our being gathered to him, we ask you, brothers, not to become easily unsettled or alarmed by some prophecy, report or letter supposed to have come from us, saying the day of the Lord has already come. Don't let anyone deceive you in any way, for that day will not come until the rebellion occurs and the man of lawlessness is revealed, the man doomed to destruction. He will oppose and will exalt himself over everything that is called God or is worshiped, so that he sets himself up in God's Temple, proclaiming himself to be God.
>
> —2 Thessalonians 2:1–4

Notice that Paul begins by reminding the Thessalonians that there is only one coming of the Lord and that the rapture is inseparable from that coming. He is obviously associating the day of the Lord with the coming of the Lord and the rapture. He then states that the day of the Lord will only come after the man of lawlessness is revealed. We know that this man, whom Scripture will reveal at that time as the Beast, will force his way into the Temple during the middle of the seven years:

> He will confirm a covenant with many for one seven. In the middle of the seven he will put an end to sacrifice and offering. And on a wing of the Temple he will set up an abomination that causes desolation, until the end that is decreed is poured out on him.
> —Daniel 9:27

Thus, the day of the Lord cannot take place until sometime after the Beast has gone into the Temple. Because the Beast had not yet been revealed as the destroyer of Israel by entering the Temple, the Thessalonians could be confident that the rapture and the day of the Lord had not yet arrived. Somehow, this Scriptural evidence has been lost by seven-year tribulationists who place the day of the Lord at the beginning of the seven years.

In 2 Thessalonians 2:5–6, Paul goes on to chide those in the church for not remembering that he had told them the sequence of end-times events when he was with them: "Don't you remember that when I was with you I used to tell you these things? And now you know what is holding him back, so that he may be revealed at the proper time." Because Paul had already told them who was holding back the man of lawlessness from being revealed, he didn't feel it was necessary to tell them again. It's unfortunate for us that he didn't tell the Thessalonians in writing, because this information would have been helpful to the nineteenth and twentieth century expositors as they were forming their concepts of eschatology.

Paul concludes by telling the Thessalonians, "For the secret power of lawlessness is already at work; but the one who holds it back will continue to do so until he is taken out of the way. And then the lawless one will be revealed" (2 Thess. 2:7–8). From this, we learn that the restraining power is an individual and that he is holding back lawlessness. When lawlessness is released, it will be personified in the Beast.

The Restraining Power

Various theories have been set forth as to who the restrainer is. Some of these include Satan, the *believing church,* human government, and the Holy Spirit. The church or human government cannot be an option, because Paul refers to the restrainer as "he." The idea of Satan being the restrainer is also not reasonable, because Satan would not have any cause to restrain evil when he is the personification of evil. For pretribulationists, the idea of the Holy Spirit being the restraining power is the best option, because this can be made to fit into their eschatology. The Holy Spirit also fits the bill because He is stronger than Satan and would be able to restrain evil.

Besides the Trinity of God, however, there is someone else whom Scripture says is stronger than Satan. In Revelation 12:7–9, we see that the archangel, Michael, the protecting angel of Israel, is at war with Satan:

> And there was war in heaven. Michael and his angels fought against the dragon, and the dragon and his angels fought back. But he was not strong enough, and they lost their place in heaven. The great dragon was hurled down—that ancient serpent called the devil, or Satan, who leads the whole world astray. He was hurled to the earth, and his angels with him.
>
> —Revelation 12:7–9

We aren't told how long the war has been in progress, but we are told that Michael is stronger than Satan. Scripture says that Michael wins the victory against Satan and hurls him down to earth. We know that this will take place during the middle of the seven years, because Scripture states it is at this time that Satan indwells the Beast, who then starts the persecution (Rev. 13:4).

Also at this time, the Beast is given forty-two months to exercise his supernatural power and authority (see Rev. 13:5). Before this event, the man called the Beast is just another ambitious politician.

Up until this time, Michael has kept Satan from attacking Israel (see Rev. 12:7–9). We know this is true because the first thing Satan does once he is loosed on the earth is wage war against Israel. From this, we can surmise that this heavenly battle represents Michael's fight to restrain Satan until the time ordained by God, at which point he stops restraining Satan and throws him down to earth. Based on this evidence, it is my conviction that Scripture is showing us that the restrainer of 2 Thessalonians 2:5–8 is Michael the archangel, not the Holy Spirit. Pretribulationists will not agree with this assessment, as the Holy Spirit has to fulfill this role in order for them to maintain their placement of the rapture as taking place before the seven-year period opens.

The Revealing of the Beast

Having been a long-time member of a church that adhered to the pretribulation theory, I had been taught for years that the Holy Spirit was the restrainer of 2 Thessalonians 2:6–7, that He indwells the church, and that, consequently, He is inseparable from the church. Therefore, the church and the Holy Spirit were to be raptured together when the Holy Spirit (the restrainer) was taken out of the way. However, if the Holy Spirit is not the restrainer, then the whole concept breaks down, and the idea of the church being raptured with the restrainer becomes unworkable. In fact, there is no association in 2 Thessalonians 2:5–8, implied or otherwise, of the church being raptured with the restrainer.

This passage also creates problems for pretribulationists in their placement of the "revealing" of the Beast at the beginning of the seven years, when he confirms the covenant with Israel. As we have already seen in 2 Thessalonians 2:3–4, the rapture takes place *after* the Beast is revealed, not before. Because the day of the Lord wrath, the coming of the Lord, and the rapture will all occur on the same day, all three events must happen within the seven years, not before. As a result, the revealing of the Beast must take place at the middle of the seven years, when he goes into the Temple and proclaims himself to be God. It is also at this point, at the middle of the seven years, that the Jews will realize that the man they thought to be their protector (as president of the EU) is not the savior they had hoped for. He is "revealed" as their destroyer. They will realize they have made a huge mistake earlier by making this covenant with death (see Isaiah 28:15). Moving the revealing of the Beast to the beginning of the seven years is thus in opposition to Scripture.

In addition, in 2 Thessalonians 2:9–10 we see that once the Beast is revealed, he will have supernatural powers:

> The coming of the lawless one will be in accordance with the work of Satan displayed in all kinds of counterfeit miracles, signs and wonders, and in every sort of evil that deceives those who are perishing.
>
> —2 Thessalonians 2:9–10

Because pretribulationists say that the Beast will be revealed at the beginning of the seven years, they are obliged to give him supernatural powers at that time. However, giving the Beast these powers at that time is putting the cart before the horse. The Beast will not receive supernatural powers with all kinds of "counterfeit miracles, signs and wonders" until he is indwelt by the supernatural Satan. This will not happen until the middle of the seven years.

The Coming of the Lord

The pretribulation placement of the rapture at the beginning of (or before) the seven years creates another problem: a coming of the Lord at the beginning of the seven years and another at the end of the seven years.

Scripture states there will be only one coming of the Lord, and that this coming will include the rapture and the day-of-the-Lord wrath. As we stated previously, this won't take place until after the Beast is revealed when he goes into the Temple in Jerusalem and claims to be God (see 2 Thess. 2:1–4).

The main reason pretribulationists insist on two comings of the Lord is because it fits with their idea that the rapture will take place before the seven years. They believe that with everything that will be going on during the second half of the seven years (i.e., persecutions, cosmic disturbances, the sign of the Son of Man in the sky), the rapture couldn't come as a thief in the night (see Matt. 24:43), as there would be a clear giveaway that something big was coming.

Based on this thinking, the elect who are gathered from the four corners of the world in Matthew 24:31 represent those whom the pretribulationists believe are saved at the end of the seven years to go into the millennial kingdom. Using 1 Thessalonians 4:13–18 as their primary text, they insist that the *first* coming of the Lord will be an invisible "coming" that takes place in the sky. Only the results will be seen—such as cars without drivers, planes without pilots, and other similar disappearances. However, it is important to note that in 1 Thessalonians 4:13–18 Paul is simply stating that the Lord will meet the church in the clouds *at the time of the rapture*. This is actually reinforced in Matthew 24:30–31, where Jesus states that He will meet His raptured church in the clouds. There is no indication that there will be two comings of the Lord.

The cosmic disturbances, sign of the Son of Man (which will be seen around the world), and the rapture depicted in Matthew 24:29–31 will take place after the persecution has been cut short. I believe these events will happen in such rapid succession that by the time unbelievers apply them to biblical fulfillment, it will be too late. It will happen just like the flood of Noah's day that came suddenly upon the unsuspecting unbelievers.

Christ's first advent was calculated from His birth to His resurrection. The second advent can be said to begin sometime during the cosmic disturbances that will take place when Christ's sign is seen in the heavens. His coming will extend *through* the rapture and the wrath of God to His actual physical touchdown at the Mount of Olives. Christ's coming could even extend for more than a year. However, there is no place in Scripture that states there will be two comings of the Lord in the last days.

The Shortening of the Persecution

In Matthew 24:21–22, Jesus, answering His disciples' questions about what would be the sign of His coming and the end of the age, says to them:

For then there will be great distress, unequaled from the beginning of the world until now—and never to be equaled again. If those days had not been cut short, no one would survive, but for the sake of the elect those days will be shortened.

The "great distress" of those days refers to the period of the Beast's persecution. However, for the most part, pretribulationists have chosen to ignore the fact that this persecution will be cut short. They do this in order for them to maintain seven years of persecution by the Beast. Marvin J. Rosenthal makes the following observations about the way many pretribulationists have misinterpreted this passage:

The Lord said, "And except those days should be shortened, there should no flesh be saved" (Matt. 24:22). This text is not speaking of universal annihilation. In Matthew 24:15–26 the topic is the abomination of desolation; the location is Israel; the participants are primarily Jews; the occasion is "the time of Jacob's (Israel's) trouble" (Jer. 30:7). It is the Jews in Israel who would perish if the Great Tribulation were not cut short. This text has frequently been taken out of context, even by gifted expositors, and used to suggest that if the Great Tribulation were not cut short, all men on earth would perish.[1]

There are many theories concerning this "shortening" of the persecution that have contributed to much of the confusion regarding the events of the end times. First, I want to establish that these last seven years (see Dan. 9:27) under discussion are the last seven years before Christ sets up His one thousand year kingdom, known as the millenniel kingdom. They are also the last seven years of the 490 years that Daniel prophesies for the nation of Israel in Daniel 9:24–27.

There are those who think that the "shortening of days" refers to taking days away from the last three and one-half years. However, this is not a possibility for the simple fact that Scripture says that the Gentiles will trample down Jerusalem for forty-two months (the last half of the seven years. See Rev. 11:2). Because God said there will be four-hundred and ninety years of punishment, no more, no less, it's obvious that God will not cut short this 490-year period of time during the last seven years. In other words, the full 490 years prophesied in Daniel 9:24 will be completed, not cut short.

Second, there are those who think that this "shortening of days" refers to the twenty-four hour day being shortened time-wise by one-third. They base this view on Revelation 8:12, which states, "The fourth angel sounded his trumpet, and a third of the sun was struck, a third of the moon, and a third of the stars, so that a third of them turned dark. A third of the day was without light, and also a third of the night." In actuality, during the wrath of God, the fourth angel will shorten each day by a third and each night by a third. This will take place after the persecution of the Beast has been cut short.

Finally, there are some who think the persecution of the Beast will be cut short because of the cosmic disturbances that will take place. They base this view on Matthew 24:29, where Jesus says, "Immediately after the distress of those days, the sun will be darkened, and the moon will not give its light." The words "immediately after" in this passage tell us that the cosmic disturbances will not overlap the persecution. Therefore, the cosmic disturbances cannot be the reason for the persecution being cut short.

In my opinion, the days of the persecution will be shortened sometime after the middle of the seven years but before the end of the seven years. Notice, we are talking about a portion of time during the last three and one-half years, not three and one-half years of persecution. Also note that nowhere in Scripture are the last seven years called the tribulation.

The Cause of the Shortening

Now that we understand the general time frame for when the shortening of the persecution will occur, we next have to examine the reason why this shortening will take place. In other words, what would make the Beast stop his persecutions during the last three and one-half years? If he still has the supernatural power to persecute the elect until the end of the seven years, what would make him end that persecution?

What I'm going to say next is studied speculation, but I believe that the answer can be found in Ezekiel 38:2–4, where God tells Ezekiel:

> Son of man, set your face against Gog, of the land of Magog, the chief prince of Meshech and Tubal; prophesy against him and say: "This is what the Sovereign LORD says: I am against you, O Gog, chief prince of Meshech and Tubal. I will turn you around, put hooks in your jaws and bring you out with your whole army—your horses, your horsemen fully armed, and a great horde with large and small shields, all of them brandishing their swords."
>
> —Ezekiel 38:2–4

At some point before the end of the *first* three and one-half years, the Lord is going to put figurative "hooks" into the jaws of the people of Magog (commonly thought to be Russia and her Muslim allies). The Lord is going to turn the people of Magog around and give them the idea of invading Israel. Their arrival in the Middle East will coincide with their Scriptural appointment at the battle of Armageddon.

After the Beast has invaded Israel during the beginning of the *last* three and one-half years (see Dan. 11:41), he will set himself up as Emperor God in the Temple at Jerusalem (see Dan. 9:27; 2 Thess. 2:4) and put his persecution into full operation. At some point during this time of persecution, he will hear an alarming report from the North and the East (undoubtedly the military mobilization of Magog, which would include the kings of the East). This will take place sometime during the *last* three and one-half years. Daniel 11:44 says that the Beast will set out in a great rage to wipe out this coming invasion of Israel. However, he must pause to mobilize his troops from all over Europe. The mobilization and deployment of troops will take some time, because his army will, no doubt, consist of every able-bodied man within his empire.

The fact that the Beast is alarmed tells us that he realizes he is facing a formidable threat that he—even with his supernatural powers—may not be able to handle. He and the False Prophet will be forced to turn their full attention to this avalanche of humanity now pouring down on them, and this distraction will leave the Beast without the time or the manpower to enforce his persecutions. This may be the cause of the cessation of the Beast's persecutions. As I said, this is just a studied speculation.

The Sign of Christ's Coming

As we previously mentioned, after the persecution of the Beast has been cut short, the cosmic disturbances will begin and the sign of the Son of Man will be seen in the sky. In Matthew 24:30–31, Jesus states the following concerning the events of this time:

> At that time the sign of the Son of Man will appear in the sky, and all the nations of the earth shall mourn. They will see the Son of Man coming on the clouds of the sky, with power and great glory. And he will send his angels with a loud trumpet call, and they will gather his elect from the four winds, from one end of the heavens to the other.
> —Matthew 24:30–31

The context of this verse indicates that the rapture will overlap with the sign of His coming but not with the persecution that has been cut short. Most likely, the "sign" that the whole world will see will be the Shekinah Glory of God, which hasn't been seen since God departed from the Temple (see Ezek. 10:18). The world will be in darkness, because the sun will not give its light (Matt. 24:29). The only light for the world at this point will be God's glory.

After this sign appears, with the voice of the archangel and a loud trumpet blast, the angels in heaven will gather the "saved" both living and dead. *This is the rapture,* and it will be the only coming of the Lord since Christ came into the world to redeem mankind from sin. The second coming will take place sometime during the last half of the seven years and will continue until Christ touches down on the Mount of Olives in Jerusalem during the battle of Armageddon.

Jesus' coming will not be silent or unseen. In Matthew 24:27, Jesus says, "For as lightning that comes from the east is visible even in the west, so will be the coming of the Son of Man." When the believing Christians are taken from the earth, no one remaining will wonder what happened to them, for the whole world will know at that time that there is a God in heaven. When the day-of-the-Lord wrath falls immediately after the rapture, the world will know from where that wrath comes. They will call on the mountains and rocks to fall on them, saying, "Hide us from the face of him who sits on the throne and from the wrath of the lamb! For the great day of their wrath has come, and who can stand?" (Rev. 6:16–17).

But how do we know that Jesus is describing the rapture in Matthew 24:31? We know because just a few verses later Jesus tells His disciples that the judgment of the flood and the salvation of Noah will parallel the judgment of the last days and the coming of the Lord:

> As it was in the days of Noah, so it will be at the coming of the Son of Man. For in the days before the flood, people were eating and drinking, marrying and giving in marriage, up to the day Noah entered the ark; and they knew nothing about what would happen until the flood came and took them all away. That is how it will be at the coming of the Son of Man. Two men will be in the field; one will be taken the other left. Two women will be grinding with a hand mill; one will be taken the other left.
>
> —Matt. 24:37–41

Notice that Jesus makes a point of saying that the flood came on the *same day* that Noah and his family entered the ark. This corresponds with the account of Noah in Genesis 7:13, which states, "On that very day Noah and his sons, Shem, Ham and Japheth, together with his wife and the wives of his three sons, entered the ark." Jesus is saying that His coming will parallel Noah's experience: the salvation of the believers (the rapture) will take place the *very same day* the wrath of God falls on an unbelieving world. What Jesus says in Matthew 24:36–41 is also reinforced by His words in Luke 17:28–29 about the salvation of Lot: "But the *day* Lot left Sodom, fire and sulfur rained down from heaven and destroyed them all." We can also see from these stories that throughout Scripture God promises that He will always rescue the righteous from His wrath.

In Matthew 24:40–41, Jesus makes sure that His point is not missed concerning the rapture when He says, "Two men will be in the field: one will be taken the other left. Two women will be grinding with a hand mill; one will be taken the other left." Some scholars, in their attempts to avoid recognizing this passage as pertaining to the rapture, insist that the "one taken" and "the other left" will take place at the judgment of the nations (see Matt. 25:31–46). They claim that one will be "taken" in judgment while the other will be left to go into the millennial kingdom. However, this interpretation takes the passage out of context. Jesus has just said that the flood judgment in the time of Noah and the wrath of God during the end times judgment are parallel. The fact that Noah and his family were saved by being taken while the rest remained for judgment parallels the event of one being taken in the rapture and the other being left for the judgment.

Pretribulation's Doctrine of Imminence

Pretribulationism has a doctrine that states the rapture is imminent. This means there is no prophetic event that must take place before the rapture. In other words, the rapture could happen at any time.

Scripture says the rapture takes place on the Day of the Lord (Matt. 24:37–41, 2 Thess. 2:1–2). Pretribulationism insists the Day of the Lord (the Wrath of God) starts at the beginning of the seven years. This insistence concerning the placement of the Day of the Lord is the major cause of contradictions within the theory of pretribulationism.

According to Scripture, certain events must take place before the rapture and the Day of the Lord. The first event is: Elijah must come before the Day of the Lord. Malachi 4:5 says, "See I will send you the prophet Elijah before that great and dreadful day of the Lord comes." This takes place in the middle of the seven years not before the seven years (Dan. 9:27).

The second event is there must be a "falling away" or "rebellion" before the rapture (2 Thess. 2:3) and the Day of the Lord.

The third event is the cutting short of the persecution. Jesus taught that the Day of the Lord would not come until after the persecution had been "cut short" (Matt. 24:29).

The fourth event is the cosmic disturbances, which occur just after the persecution is shortened. They are seen taking place just before the Day of the Lord in Joel 2:31, Revelation 6:12 and Matthew 24:29.

An Arbitrary Gap of Time

When confronted with the fact of the pre-Day of the Lord events just discussed, pretribulationists attempt to avoid conflict with Scripture by placing an arbitrary time gap between the rapture and the signing of the covenant with Israel (which they say reveals the Beast and starts the Day of the Lord wrath). They say this hypothetical time gap could be a day, a month, or several years. They are correct in saying that it is the signing of the covenant, and not the rapture, that starts the seven-years. But then they insert an arbitrary time gap between the rapture and the signing of the covenant, which then makes allowance for the pre-Day of the Lord events to come after the rapture, but before the Day of the Lord.

On the other hand, they have maintained through the years (according to their interpretation of 2 Thessalonians 2:6–8) that the Holy Spirit and the Church are raptured at the time the Beast is revealed. By making the claim that the Beast is revealed when he signs the covenant with Israel and that the Holy Spirit is removed along with the Church (raptured) their "gap" theory does not stand. Within their own theory, there is this contradiction that doesn't allow for any kind of a time gap between the signing of the covenant and the rapture. Consequently, the pre-Day of the Lord events (see Scriptural events listed above) still remain before the rapture. The rapture cannot be imminent when confronted with the Scriptural evidence.

Had pretribulationism not made the entire seven years a time of God's Wrath, thus, forcing the starting the Day of the Lord at the beginning of the seven years, their manipulation of end-times events would not be necessary. The house of pretribulationism crumbles when all the Scriptural data is compared and evaluated.

Reservations Cancelled

Some who do not subscribe to the pre-wrath theory believe that if the rapture were to take place late in the last three and one-half years, it wouldn't leave time for the judgment of the deeds of the believer (see 1 Cor. 3:13, Rev. 22:12) and the marriage of the Lamb in heaven (see Rev. 19:7–9). However, we have to remember that by this point the church will be in eternity, which means it will be out of the confines of time as we know it. The events taking place in heaven after the rapture might happen within a millisecond if they were viewed within our frame of reference of time and space. We have little concept of eternity.

Another reservation about this placement of a pre-wrath rapture in the last half of the seven years is: There would not be enough time for more people to be saved under the gospel of the kingdom to go into the millennial kingdom. The millennial kingdom is defined as Christ's ruling the earth for a thousand years after the battle of Armageddon. The people who will occupy this kingdom in the beginning will be people who have received Christ through the gospel of the kingdom between the rapture and the judgment of the nations (see Matt. 25:31–46). These people will live in their natural bodies, and will have children who may or may not follow the Lord during their life times. However, we know that there will be at least five months after the rapture takes place until the battle of Armageddon begins. Revelation 9:10 tells us that locusts, which look like horses and have tails that sting like scorpions, will torment people for five months during the time of the wrath of God. This demonic attack will take place at the fifth of the seven trumpet judgments and during the seventh seal (see Rev. 9:1–11). So if this judgment lasts five months and takes place during the fifth trumpet, who is to say how long the other judgments will last? That is why I say that the Lord's coming could last for as long as a year. And even if the time left after the rapture were only the Scriptural minimum of five months, it would still be enough time for thousands to find salvation through the gospel of the kingdom and be counted worthy to go into the millennial kingdom.

The Implications

In conclusion, consider for a moment some of the implications of the rapture taking place on the day-of-the-Lord wrath:

- The church will witness the covenant the Beast confirms with Israel.
- The church will be on earth for the persecution, which will only take place in Europe and around the Mediterranean area.
- The church outside of Europe will have to stand by helplessly as thousands of Christians and Jews in the Beast's empire are slaughtered. (There may be some connection here to what Jesus

says in Matthew 25:32–33 regarding the sheep and goats and believers' attempt, or non-attempt, to help Christ's "brothers.")

- The church will be on earth as the EU mobilizes its forces and the Russian, Islamic, and Eastern nations prepare their troops for the Battle of Armageddon.
- The church will see the cosmic disturbances and the Shekinah glory as it lights up a darkened sky.
- The church will be raptured before the wrath of God overtakes a sin-sick world.

Imagine with me the moment of the rapture. Immediately, we are in the presence of the God of the universe, who placed the stars in space and who also knows each one of us by name. Then, and only then, will we have some idea of the cost He paid to redeem us from sin. When we see His glory and witness His exulted position, we will, without a doubt, be so overwhelmed that it will be incomprehensible to us how He, in His love and mercy, could set it all aside to take on the pain of human flesh to save sinners from the eternal fires. With grateful hearts, we will kneel before Him. "Amazing love! How can it be, that Thou, my God, should die for me?"[2]

Summary

The rapture will take place on the same day that the day-of-the-Lord wrath falls. That day will be just after the Beast's persecution has been cut short. Cosmic disturbances will occur, and the sign of the Son of Man will be seen throughout the world. There will be a loud trumpet blast, and the Lord will send out His angels to collect all the saved from the four corners of the world. Aside from Christ's first advent, this will be the one and only coming of the Lord.

It is important to understand the timing of the rapture, because we have been called to serve as witnesses to God's coming judgment. We have been warned through God's Word of "things not yet seen," and we must act to warn a lost world of God's provision of salvation. In Matthew 24:44, Jesus says, "the Son of Man will come at an hour when you [referring to unbelievers] do not expect him." As Christians, we have been given the general time frame for when the rapture and the day-of-the-Lord wrath will take place (though not the exact day, or hour), and we need to warn others that the judgment is coming.

In 2 Thessalonians 2:3–4, Paul wrote that the day of the Lord would not come "until the rebellion occurs and the man of lawlessness [the Beast] is revealed, the man doomed to destruction. He will oppose and will exalt himself over everything that is called God or is worshiped, so that he sets himself up in God's Temple, proclaiming himself to be God." The day of the Lord thus cannot take place until sometime after the Beast has gone into the Temple.

Paul also states that there is a "restraining force" holding back Satan from attacking Israel (see 2 Thess. 2:7–8). Many theories exist as to who this person is, but we know from Scripture that the archangel, Michael, the protecting angel of Israel, is at war with Satan and has the power to hold him back. At the middle of the seven years, at a time appointed by God, Michael will stop restraining Satan and throw him down to earth. This will be the time Satan indwells the Beast, who will then be given forty-two months to exercise his supernatural power (see Rev. 13:5). The Beast, whom the Jews thought was their protector, will be "revealed" instead as their destroyer.

Once the Beast sets himself up as Emperor God in the Temple, his persecutions will be in full operation. In Matthew 24:21–22, however, Jesus says that this time of persecution will be "cut short." There are many theories about what this "shortening" means, but it most likely refers to the number of days of persecution being shortened some time after the middle of the seven years. The cause of this shortening could likely be the mobilization of "Magog" (Russia and her Muslim allies) against the forces of the Beast. The Beast will be alarmed, and this distraction will cause him to cut short his persecutions.

In Matthew 24:30–31, Jesus told His disciples, "The Son of Man will appear in the sky … and he will send his angels with a loud trumpet call, and they will gather his elect from the four winds, from one end of the heavens to the other." We can be assured that He is describing the rapture in this passage, because He then compares the experience of Noah and his family being saved out of the judgment of the flood to the salvation of the saints being saved from the end-times judgment.

Jesus confirms in Matthew 24:22 that His coming, the rapture, and the day-of-the-Lord wrath will take place after the persecution has been cut short.

CHAPTER 6

THE FOUR GREAT BEASTS OF THE APOCALYPSE

In Ezekiel 37, God brought Ezekiel to a valley filled with dry bones. He told the prophet that the bones represented the house of Israel during the last days. He then said, "O my people, I am going to open your graves and bring you up from them; I will bring you back to the land of Israel" (Ezek. 37:12).

I believe that the nation of Israel is God's barometer of the end times. Since the formation of Israel in 1948, we have witnessed these bones of Ezekiel's vision returning to Israel out of the ghetto graves of Europe. However, at this time, these "bones" have no breath in them, which means they are returning as a secular nation and have not yet been filled with the Spirit of God. Yet, there will be another great ingathering of Jews to Israel after the battle of Armageddon, and at that time, they will all be filled with the Spirit of God and know the Lord (Hosea 3:5). The prophet Jeremiah wrote:

> This is what the LORD, the God of Israel, says: "Write in a book all the words I have spoken to you. The days are coming," declares the LORD, "when I will bring my people Israel and Judah back from

captivity and restore them to the land I gave their forefathers to possess," says the Lord.

—Jeremiah 30:3

As we mentioned in chapter one, after almost 2,500 years of being scattered throughout the Gentile nations, Israel again became a nation on May 14, 1948. This was God's clue to us that "the times of the Gentiles" (Luke 21:24) were drawing to a close.

As we also stated, many of the most influential works regarding end-times prophecy were written during the early part of the 1900s. Because these works were written before this important event occurred, the expositors did not have all of the pieces to properly understand the symbolism in biblical prophecy and thus have contributed to, in my opinion, a very serious misinterpretation concerning the four beasts of Daniel 7. In this chapter, I will attempt to explain, which I believe to be misconceptions, and show why the interpretations of many of these early biblical expositors were incorrect.

The Unsealing

Daniel 7 has always been a pivotal chapter in the consideration of end-times prophecy. The *Homiletic Commentary* makes the following comment concerning this chapter in Daniel:

> This chapter, in its matter as well as its position in the central part of the book, is to the book of Daniel what the eighth chapter of Romans is to that epistle. Next to the fifty-third chapter of Isaiah and perhaps the ninth chapter also, we have here the most precious and prominent portions of the sure word of prophecy concerning the coming of the Messiah. This chapter is worthy of the most careful prayer and study. It is referred to directly or indirectly by Christ and his apostles perhaps more than any other portion of the Old Testament of similar extent. It appears to have been regarded by Old Testament saints in the centuries preceding the Messiah's first advent, as pre-eminently the "word of prophecy."[1]

In Daniel 12:4, according to the translators of the King James Version, the angel said to Daniel, "But thou, O Daniel, shut up the words, and seal the book, even to the time of the end: many shall run to and fro, and knowledge shall be increased." This was a regrettable translation, as it has caused many to preach and write about how the end times are upon us because speed and knowledge have increased during the last 100 years. The truth is that even though speed and knowledge have increased at an incredible rate, this is not what this verse is referring to.

The Amplified Bible renders a more exact meaning: "But you, O Daniel, shut up the words and seal the book until the time of the end. (Then) many shall run to and fro and search anxiously (through the book), and knowledge (of God's purposes as revealed by His prophets) shall be increased and become great." In other words, at the time of the end, the book of Daniel will be unsealed by world events. God's people will make the connection of these events with the time of the end and will search anxiously through God's Word. By so doing, the knowledge of God's purposes will be revealed and will be greatly increased (Dan. 12:4).

Are we living in the days of Daniel's prophecies? I believe that many prophecy watchers of today have not recognized that we are because they are basing their interpretation of biblical events on the opinions of expositors who wrote their commentaries before the historic events of 1948. This is especially true regarding the prophecies in Daniel 7.

Again, it is important to remember that the times of the Gentiles began when the Temple in Jerusalem was destroyed in 586 B.C. and the Jews went into the Babylonian captivity. From that time on, Israel did not control the Promised Land. As we saw from Daniel's interpretation of King Nebuchadnezzar's dream in Daniel 2:36–45, biblical prophecy stated that there would be four empires plus a revival of the fourth empire that would negatively impact the nation of Israel. These empires were Babylon, Medo-Persia, Greece, Rome, and Rome in its revived form as the EU.

I believe the expositors of the 1800s and 1900s mistakenly interpreted the beasts of Daniel 7 to be the same as the above ancient empires. Since then, many Bible students have followed in their footsteps, and many influential individuals and organizations have also accepted this interpretation. In fact, most of the Bibles I have seen that offer commentary on passages of Scripture presume that the beasts in Daniel 7 directly relate to the four metals used in the image in Nebuchadnezzar's dream in Daniel 2.

Of course, there are a few Bible scholars who have not bought into this theory. David Hocking, in his book *Dare to Be a Daniel*, casts a long shadow of doubt over the ancient empire theory of the four beasts. Noah Hutchings, of South West Radio Church fame, also refutes this theory in his book *Daniel*. In his magazine *Zion's Fire*, Marvin Rosenthal has written that he believes the four beasts are the modern-nation equivalent of the four ancient empires; that is, Babylon is Iraq, Persia is Iran, Greece is Syria (the Syrian fourth of Alexander the Great's Greek Empire), and the Roman Empire is the European Union.

The late Dr. Henry M. Morris perhaps came the closest to identifying the four beasts. In his book *The Revelation Record*, in my opinion, he not only correctly identifies the problem of equating the four beasts in Daniel 7 to ancient empires, but also he takes into account the Scriptural description of the beasts, which most expositors fail to do. He writes:

> It is usual to interpret the four beasts of Daniel 7 as the historical Empires of Babylonia, Medo-Persia, Greece and Rome, in order. This corresponds precisely to the meaning of the four parts of the image of Nebuchadnezzar's dream in Daniel 2. Practically all Bible scholars agree on this, and the contextual chapters of Daniel confirm it at least as far as the three empires are concerned, and as far as Nebuchadnezzar's image is concerned.
>
> However, there are difficulties in applying the same interpretation to the beasts of Daniel 7. Although they do appear in order, the four beasts seem to be contemporaneous rather than sequential. The four appear first in correspondence to the parallel statement: Behold, the four winds of heaven strove upon the great sea (Dan. 7:2). Furthermore, all four beasts continue to strive with each other until the end; in fact, the lives of the first three beasts were prolonged for a season and a time after the fourth beast had his body destroyed, and given to the burning flame (Dan. 7:11–12). Finally, all four beasts were still future at the time of Daniel's writing (Dan. 7:17), even though at the time Babylonia had already fallen and Medo-Persia had come into dominance.

Thus, it seems probable that the four beasts of Daniel 7 represent four great kingdoms (or possibly confederations), one each from the North, South, East and West, like the four winds striving over the sea. The beast of the West (the lion with eagle's wings) might, for example, represent the British lion and the American eagle, for the Western alliance in general. The second is the great devouring bear, which could well be the Russian Colossus and her communist satellites. The third is a four-headed, four winged leopard, possibly symbolizing a future Eastern Alliance.[2]

With all due respect to Dr. Morris, I believe these four beasts are in sequence, as well as, being contemporaries. In addition, I also believe (for reasons I will state in the following sections) that he is incorrect in stating that the fourth beast is thrown into the blazing fire and that Babylon had fallen at the time of Daniel's vision of the beasts. However, Dr. Morris does accurately point out that the beasts in Daniel 7 have no parallel with Daniel 2 and that these beasts refer to nations in our time.

What Went Wrong?

It's not difficult to understand how the early expositors made this error. The fourth kingdom of Daniel 7 has ten horns; the statue of Daniel 2 has ten toes. The fourth kingdom of Daniel 7 has teeth of iron; the statue of Daniel 2 has toes made of iron and clay. The ten-toed kingdom in Daniel 2 is the last kingdom before Christ's return; the ten-horn kingdom in Daniel 7 is the last empire before Christ's return. Based on this evidence, it must have seemed obvious to them that the fourth beast of Daniel 7 represented the fourth empire of the statue of Daniel 2 (ancient Rome). They were half-way correct in making this assumption; however, using the fourth beast as a benchmark, they then went on to assume that the other three beasts of Daniel 7 were the ancient empires of Babylon, Medo-Persia, and Greece.[3]

These expositors were so convinced that they had come to the correct conclusion that they stopped looking for collaborating evidence about these four beasts in Scripture. Had they not stopped at this point, they would have seen that the four beasts represent modern nations, even though they would not have known the names of those nations. Their efforts remind me of the story of the airplane pilot who was flying in the dark and didn't believe his instruments. He made his own adjustments to compensate for what he thought was a correct altitude and ended up crashing his plane in a desert.

By ignoring the evidence, these expositors also falsely concluded that the ten horns would be destroyed at Christ's return, because in the vision in Daniel 2 the toes are crushed by the stone that comes out of heaven. This idea was seemingly confirmed for them when they turned to Daniel 7:11–12:

> Then I continued to watch because of the boastful words the horn was speaking. I kept looking until the beast was slain and its body destroyed and thrown into the blazing fire. The other beasts had been stripped of their authority, but were allowed to live for a period of time.

When they saw the beast in this passage being thrown into the blazing fire, they surmised that this beast was the fourth beast (empire) of Daniel 7:7:

> After that, in my vision at night I looked, and there before me was a fourth beast—terrifying and frightening and very powerful. It had iron teeth; it crushed and devoured its victims and trampled underfoot whatever was left. It was different from all the former beasts, and it had ten horns.

They then had to search for an explanation as to how the lion, the bear, and the four-headed leopard (which they thought were the ancient empires of Babylon, Medo-Persia, and Greece) could go on living after the fourth beast of Daniel 7:7 was thrown into the fire. They concluded that each beast's ancient culture was assimilated by each successive conquering empire. In other words, Babylon's culture was assimilated by Medo-Persia; Medo-Persia's culture was assimilated by Greece; and then all four cultures came together in the Roman empire and will go on living until the fourth beast (the Roman Empire) is finally destroyed.

So, because they incorrectly believed that the fourth beast would be thrown into the fire, they assumed the other beast's have passed into history. Only their cultures go on living until the fourth beast is thrown into the fire. The following quote from *Jamison, Fausset and Brown's Commentary on the Whole Bible* is typical of their ideas:

> "The rest of the beasts" i.e., the three first, had passed away not by direct destroying judgments, such as consumed the little horn, as being the final matured evil of the fourth beast. They continued to exist, but their "dominion was taken away," whereas the fourth beast shall cease utterly, superseded by the Messiah's kingdom.[4]

By saying that the first three beasts "had passed away," the early expositors relegated them to ancient history without really explaining how the beasts could go on living. They cast the fourth empire of Daniel 7 into the role of the beast that is thrown into the Lake of Fire. In actuality, it is the little-horn beast that is thrown into the Lake of Fire.

The beast that is destroyed in Daniel 7:11 is not the fourth beast of Daniel 7:7 (an empire) but the "little horn beast" of Daniel 7:8 (a man). This beast is called a "little horn" until Daniel 7:11, when his name changes to "the beast" (Beast). His name is changed because it is at this point that he (the little horn who speaks boastfully) is judged. The Lord Jesus then takes away his horn (his power and authority) and throws him into the blazing fire. When this occurs, he reverts back to his role as the Beast. Only individuals, never empires or nations, are thrown into the blazing fire.

The Evidence Uncovered

I believe there are several problems with these early expositors' conclusions that the four beasts represent ancient empires. First, as previously mentioned, the empires in Nebuchadnezzar's dream in Daniel 2 are symbolic representations of the Gentile world system during "the times of the Gentiles." The ten-toed kingdom is the culmination of this Gentile world system, and when it is replaced by the Kingdom of God, it collapses and is seen no more. In contrast, all four beasts in

Daniel 7 go on living as nations without authority after the battle of Armageddon (see Dan. 7:9–12). This tells us that we are viewing two entirely different events.

In addition, each empire depicted in Daniel 2 conquers the preceding one. However, in Daniel 7, the four beasts are said to remain and be sovereign until sometime after the Beast is thrown into the blazing fire (see Dan. 7:11–12). The four beasts in Daniel 7 are contemporaries of one another and do not destroy each other as do the four metallic empires in Daniel 2. Again, this shows us that we are viewing two separate events.

Note also that Daniel wrote the prophecy in Daniel 7 during the first year of Belshazzar, the last king of Babylon. By this time, Nebuchadnezzar had been dead for many years, and Babylon's status as an empire was just about to pass into history. (As you might remember, according to Daniel 5, it was Belshazzar who quaked at the sight of the handwriting on the wall, which took place the very night Babylon fell to the Medes.) The angel, interpreting Daniel's vision, said to him, "The four great beasts are four kingdoms that *will rise* from the earth" (Dan. 7:17, emphasis mine). The use of the future tense "will rise" places all four beasts in the future. Consequently, Babylon cannot be the lion beast. That being true, it follows that the bear cannot be Medo-Persia and the leopard cannot be ancient Greece.

Some students of prophecy claim that the story of Nebuchadnezzar in Daniel 4 shows that Babylon is the lion. In Daniel 4:16, Nebuchadnezzar was driven away from men because of his pride. While under this punishment from God, he ate grass like cattle, grew hair like feathers, and developed claws like a bird. Seven years later, he was restored to his position as king of Babylon. The description of the creature that Nebuchadnezzar became only matches the lion of Daniel 7 in that he lived as a wild animal for seven years. His description in Daniel 4 is more like a bird than a lion.

This idea of Nebuchadnezzar becoming like a lion was reinforced when a depiction of a lion with wings with the bust of Nebuchadnezzar was discovered on a building in ancient Babylon (see Dan. 7:4). However, in the story of Nebuchadnezzar in Daniel 4, the king was not given the heart of a beast and then later given the heart of a man, as the prophecy in Daniel 7:4 indicates is true of the lion. Scripture just says that Nebuchadnezzar was sent away to live as an animal for seven years, and then seven years later was restored to his kingdom. The story does not even point to a conclusion that Nebuchadnezzar became a lion. When did we ever hear of a lion eating grass? The only time lions will eat grass is during the millennial kingdom.

The argument that the four-headed leopard is the Greek Empire of Alexander is also difficult to maintain. We know from history that after Alexander's death, his empire was divided into four geographical areas by four of his generals. However, if the four heads of the leopard represent Alexander's four generals, it would mean that the beast represents a fractured and declining Greek Empire. If Nebuchadnezzar was identified as the head of Babylon, wouldn't we expect Alexander the Great (and not his generals) to represent the head of the leopard?

Scripture is exact and makes no mistakes. Daniel 8:8, which does refer to Alexander and his generals, states, "The goat became very great, but at the height of his power his large horn was broken off, and in its place four prominent horns grew up towards the four winds of heaven." The large horn that was broken off was Alexander, and Scripture credits him as being the head of the Greek Empire. It thus stands to reason that he would also be seen as its head in Daniel 7 if the leopard were in fact the Greek Empire. Furthermore, in Daniel 7:6, the leopard is given authority to rule. This statement cannot refer to the Greek Empire, as Alexander was never given such authority. He took the known world at that time by force.

If the goat in Daniel 8:8 and the leopard in Daniel 7:6 both represent the Greek Empire, it would mean that Scripture has used two different animals to represent the same entity. Could it be that the Lord would confuse the issue by changing the symbols, or can we still rely on one of the basic rules of interpretation that states Scripture will interpret Scripture? I maintain that this rule is valid and that the lion is not Babylon and the bear and leopard beasts are not Medo-Persia and Greece, respectively, but modern nations.

The fourth beast in Daniel 7:7–8 is identified with the empires of Greece and Rome. The fourth beast, with the ten horns, has two metal parts on its body: (1) teeth of iron, which identify it with the legs of iron of the statue (Rome), and (2) nails of brass (see Dan. 7:19), which identify it with the belly and thighs of brass (Greece). Scripture identifies the fourth beast with the two metals of the statue because both this beast in Daniel 7 and the Greek Empire are involved with "little horns."

The first "little horn" is believed to be Antiochus Epiphanes, who later ruled the Syrian fourth of Alexander's Greek empire (the belly and thighs of brass). After conquering Israel around 165 B.C., this first "little horn" desecrated the Temple in Jerusalem by offering swine on the altar of sacrifice.

The second "little horn" is the Beast (the ruler of the revived Roman Empire), who will also desecrate the Temple, starting the period known as "Jacob's Trouble" (the persecution) in the last days. The ten-horned beast has a similarity to the Greek Empire by having nails of brass, which identifies it with Antiochus Epiphanes, the first "little horn." Shouldn't we expect to see some brass on the leopard if it were the Greek Empire?

Finally, in Daniel 7:15–16, we read that Daniel was troubled in his understanding about these four beasts. Why would he be troubled if these four beasts represented the same entities that God had revealed to him in Nebuchadnezzar's dream?

A One-World Government?

Based on this overwhelming evidence, one must conclude that the four beasts of Daniel 7 represent modern nations. Since this is true, it reveals another important fact concerning the end times: each of the four beasts is an *independent nation* and will remain sovereign until the time of the judgment of the nations after the battle of Armageddon. Their sovereignty is indicated by the fact that the Lord God will strip the authority to rule away from three of the beasts but will allow them to continue on as nations (see Dan. 7:12). If these nations were not sovereign, the Lord would only have to take the authority to rule away from the Beast. This points to the fact that there will *not* be a one-world government on earth before Jesus sets up His millennial kingdom, as many prophecy experts have claimed.

For years, we have heard reports about how multinational, clandestine organizations have been scheming to bring in a one-world government. With globalization pressuring the world's economy and the World Trade Organization's insistence on conformity of nations, the United Nation's attempts to grab power to its self, it doesn't take much to convince us that these reports are true. In fact, most who hold to the teachings of the popular prophecy media today have been so influenced by these reports that they believe a one-world government is just around the corner.

There are many different ideas and elaborate scenarios given for how this one-world government will come into being. One group maintains that the world will go into financial chaos and that when the Beast comes up with a worldwide solution to this crisis, every nation will unite under his leadership. Some pretribulationists believe that the disappearance of millions of Christians during the rapture will serve to bring all the nations of the world together. There are others who suggest that the United Nations will be the source of this unifying force or that the outbreak of war will cause the nations on the earth to rally around the Beast. Then there are those who adhere to the theory that the Beast will die from a blow to the head. They claim that the world will be so amazed at his resurrection that they will promote him to be the ruler of the world. Still others believe what is known as the "club of Rome" scenario. This "club" is supposedly made up of the movers and shakers of multinational organizations and is said to have already divided up the world into ten regions of control.

Those who believe that a one-world government will come together during the rule of the Beast quote Revelation 13 as their biblical source. And, in fact, it cannot be denied that parts of Revelation 13 do seem to indicate that there will be a one-world government during Daniel's seventieth seven. The following verses appear to provide ample proof that such a government will take place:

> One of the heads of the beast seemed to have had a fatal wound, but the fatal wound had been healed. The whole world was astonished and followed the beast.... He was given power to make war against the saints and to conquer them. And he was given authority over

every tribe, people, language and nation. All inhabitants of the earth will worship the beast.... Then I saw another beast, coming out of the earth. He had two horns like a lamb, but he spoke like a dragon. He exercised all the authority of the first beast on his behalf, and made the earth and its inhabitants worship the first beast.... He also forced everyone, small and great, rich and poor, free and slave, to receive a mark on his right hand or on his forehead, so that no one could buy or sell unless he had the mark.

— Revelation 13:3; 7–8; 11–12; 16–17

Of course, in order to verify the claim that these verses indicate a one-world government will come into being before Jesus returns and sets up the millennial kingdom, one must first examine Scripture to see if there is any evidence to the contrary. As we have seen, Daniel 7:12 provides this evidence, for it seems logical to conclude that because three of the four beasts will not be under the control of the Beast before or after this judgment, they will be sovereign during the time of the last seven years—a period when some say the Beast is supposed to rule the entire world. Thus, we have to conclude that the Beast doesn't rule the entire world at any time.

Revelation 6:8 indicates the Beast and the False Prophet only rule over one fourth of the world, which I maintain is the Old Roman Empire territory:

"I looked, and there before me was a pale horse! Its rider was named, Death, and Hades was following close behind him. They were given power over a fourth of the earth to kill by sword, famine and the wild beasts of the earth."

Whole or Part?

The seeming discrepancy between Revelation 13 (where it is said that the Beast will rule the whole world) and Daniel 7 (where it is seen that the Beast does not rule the entire world) must be reconciled. We know that Scripture does not contradict itself. Therefore, I submit for your consideration that the words "every," "whole," and "all" in the context of Revelation 13 do not necessarily mean the *whole* world but only a localized area, such as the "whole world" known to the writer of that particular portion of Scripture. We find evidence to support this conclusion in Luke 2:1, where the phrase "whole world" in the *King James Version* is translated "the entire Roman world" in the *New International Version*. Other examples from Scripture also indicate that the Hebrew and Greek words for "whole world" or "whole earth" have the possibility of multiple meanings, such as a localized area, region, or country:

- "And *all the countries* came to Egypt to buy grain from Joseph, because the famine was severe in *all the whole earth*" (Gen. 41:57, emphasis mine).
- "This day the Lord will hand you over to me, and I will strike you down and cut off your head. Today I will give the carcasses of the Philistine army to the birds of the air and the beasts of the earth, and the *whole world* will know that there is a God in Israel" (1 Sam. 17:46, emphasis mine).
- "The *whole world* sought audience with Solomon to hear the wisdom God had put in his heart" (1 Kings 10:24, emphasis mine).
- "After you, another kingdom will rise, inferior to yours. Next a third kingdom, one of bronze, will rule over *the whole earth*" (Dan. 2:39, emphasis mine).
- "On that day, when *all the nations of the earth* are gathered against her [Jerusalem], I will make Jerusalem an immovable rock for *all the nations*. All who try to move it will injure themselves" (Zech. 12:3, emphasis mine).
- "So the Pharisees said to one another, 'See, this is getting us nowhere. Look how the *whole world* has gone after him!'" (John 12:19, emphasis mine).

All of these quotes are from writers or speakers who had a limited world view or perspective of the world. Likewise, if we view the idea of the "whole world" in Revelation 13 as a localized, revived Roman world, the discrepancies between this passage and Daniel 7 disappear.

Problems Dissolve

Other major problems concerning end-times events can be solved if we assume that the "whole world" in Revelation 13 refers only to a localized revived Roman world. For example, Scripture indicates that there will be other nations that don't come under the Beast's control during the last three and one-half years (Dan. 11:41). For the most part, these passages of Scripture have been ignored because Bible commentators weren't sure what to do with the idea of countries not coming under the domination of the Beast. As we have stated, because of what is said in Revelation 13, the mindset of most futurist commentators has been that the Beast will rule the entire world.

Let's look at Daniel 11:42, where the angel tells Daniel, "He [the Beast] will extend his power over *many countries*" (emphasis mine). From this, we can surmise that the Beast's power will not be extended over all countries of the world, just over many. Daniel 11:41 says, "Many countries will fall, but Edom, Moab and the leaders of Ammon will be delivered from his hand." Again, we have the limiting word "many" in this verse. Because Edom and Moab are now part of Jordan, with Ammon as the capital, we have in this passage a direct statement that the nation of Jordan will not come under the Beast's control. This is why I believe the Beast will only control Western Europe and a few nations around the Mediterranean Sea.

The prophet Ezekiel may shed some light on this idea of the Beast's not ruling the entire world. In Ezekiel 38:14–16, he writes:

> Therefore son of man, prophesy and say to Gog: "This is what the sovereign Lord says: In that day, when my people Israel are living in safety, will you not take notice of it? You will come from your place in the far North, you and many nations with you, all of them riding on horses, a great horde, a mighty army. You will advance against my people Israel like a cloud that covers the land. In days to come, O Gog, I will bring you against my land, so that the nations may know me when I show myself holy through you before their eyes."

In this passage, Ezekiel the prophet is saying that in the last days, Gog, the ruler of Magog (thought to be Russia), will invade Israel with a great army that includes many other nations. I believe this refers to the battle of Armageddon. If the Beast is supposed to rule the whole world at this time, then why do Magog and her allies appear to be sovereign?

In addition, the rulers who are called to the battle of Armageddon aren't referred to as satraps or governors. They are called "kings" (see Rev. 16:16), a title that implies sovereignty. The same applies to the kings who mourn the destruction of Babylon (see Rev. 18:9).

Some attempt to justify their claim of a one-world government by stating that these sovereign nations that come against the Beast have rebelled against him just before the battle of Armageddon. This rebellion would also allow them to be sovereign after the battle of Armageddon. The problem with this claim is that there is nothing in Scripture that even hints of such a rebellion of the nations. A rebellion of this magnitude during the last days would be so significant that it surely would have been included in Scripture if it were true.

Another huge problem for the one-world government theory is the idea of the mark of the Beast being forced on the world of Islam. As we previously mentioned, those of the Islamic faith would never swear allegiance to a Western leader who is not a Muslim, much less worship him. In the middle of the seven years, when the mark of the Beast is forced on those in the Beast's empire, it will mean not only the death of millions of Jews and Christians but also the deaths of millions in the Islamic faith (there are approximately 54 million Muslims in Europe, and growing, at the time of this writing) who will live under the Beast's control. The mark could never be forced on the world of Islam outside of the Beast's empire without a major war, which, I'm sure, would have been noted in Scripture. It is my conviction that the bottom line is: a one-world government will *never* be a reality before Jesus returns to set up His millennial kingdom.

The Problem of Complacency

The idea of a one-world government system has led to a feeling of complacency among Christians. This complacency has been exacerbated by a false sense of security that the church will not go through what some believe to be seven years of persecution. The thought persists among Christians that everything will be business as usual for a long time, and that even if it isn't, they will be taken in the rapture and won't be on earth to have to worry about it. I believe that thought is a lie from Satan. Although the church for the most part will not be included in the persecution of the Beast, it will be present on earth to witness it.

The point is that there will not be a period of watching and waiting to see if this one-world government comes together before the events of the end times come upon us. Jacques Delors, by becoming president of the European Union, has fulfilled the prophecy of Revelation 17:12–13, and the time of the end may be closer than many of us realize. With the facts before us, it may therefore be wise for us to reevaluate our belief system concerning the end times and take inventory of our spiritual status with God.

Summary

We are living in the time of the "unsealing" of the book of Daniel—a time God's Word indicates will usher in the end times. However, many prophecy watchers have not recognized this fact because they are basing their interpretations of biblical prophecies on the opinions of nineteenth and twentieth century expositors who formulated their ideas before this unsealing took place.

One of the primary misinterpretations these expositors made was in depicting the four beasts in Daniel 7 as ancient empires instead of modern nations. There is no Scriptural evidence that indicates the four beasts refer to ancient empires. Some of the arguments as to why this is the case include the following:

1. The four beasts appear one after the other and are all on the scene together after the "little horn" beast is thrown into the fire. They do not destroy each other, as do the empires of Daniel 2, but are contemporary with each other. Because they are living nations, lacking only the authority to rule, they cannot be ancient empires. Also, empires are never thrown into the Lake of Fire, only individuals. This dictates that it is the little horn Beast who is thrown into the fire.

2. Daniel receives the vision of Daniel 7 at the *end* of the Babylonian Empire. The angel, in speaking to Daniel about the four beasts, uses the future tense "will rise" in Daniel 7:17, which places the beasts in the future and beyond the ancient empire of Babylon.

3. In the story of Nebuchadnezzar in Daniel 4, the king lives as a creature of the field. Some offer this as evidence the king has become like a lion. However, the lion in Daniel 7 was a beast from the beginning, and a man's heart was "given" to it, not "restored" to it. In addition, there is no mention of or reference made to Nebuchadnezzar being a lion in Daniel 4.

4. It is difficult to believe that the four-headed leopard represents the Greek Empire of Alexander the Great at its zenith, because there is 'no single head' on the leopard to represent Alexander.

5. Scripture identifies the ram and the shaggy goat as Medo-Persia and the Greek Empire, respectively, in Daniel 8. Some interpreters use this arbitrarily to cast the identity of the bear in Daniel 7 as Medo-Persia and the leopard as Greece. In doing so, they are denying a general rule of interpretation that states Scripture will interpret itself by Scripture.

6. Daniel 7:6 says the leopard "was given authority to rule." Alexander was never given authority to rule; he took whatever he wanted by force.

7. The fourth beast with the ten horns has two metal parts on its body: (1) teeth of iron, which identify it with the legs of iron of the statue (Rome), and (2) nails of brass (see Dan. 7:19), which identify it with the belly and thighs of brass (Greece). However, the leopard has no brass on its body. If the leopard represented the Greek Empire, shouldn't it have brass somewhere on its body?

8. In Daniel 7:15–16, Daniel himself doesn't seem to know who the beasts are. If these beasts are the same empires as in Daniel 2, as expositors claim, then one would assume that Daniel would not be questioning the identity of the beasts.

Daniel 7:11–12 states, "The other beasts had been stripped of their authority, but were allowed to live for a period of time." If the four beasts of Daniel 7 represent modern nations, we can surmise that these four kingdoms (beasts) will be sovereign until the Lord Jesus takes away their individual authority to rule, which will occur after the battle of Armageddon. This discounts the one-world government theory, for if the Beast ruled the whole world, the Lord would only need to remove the authority to rule from the Beast before throwing him into the flames.

The Beast only rules over the fourth kingdom. Because the other three kingdoms are sovereign after the battle of Armageddon, each kingdom must have been sovereign during the last seven years. If the first three beasts do not come under the authority of the Beast at any time, it's reasonable to assume that other nations of the world (with the exception of members of the EU) also will not come under the Beast's control.

Finally, there appears to be a discrepancy between this prophecy in Daniel 7 and that in Revelation 13, which seems to imply that the Beast will take over the "whole world." However, if one considers that the phrase "whole world" could apply only to the localized area known to the writer at that time, this discrepancy disappears. The verses in Revelation 13 that say the Beast will rule "all the world" must refer to a limited world, such as the entire old Roman Empire.

Therefore, there will not be a one-world government before Christ returns, and Christians should not be lulled into a false sense of security that the end times are not upon us because such a system has not yet come into place.

CHAPTER 7

THE IDENTITY OF THE FOUR BEASTS

As we have seen, the four beasts of Daniel 7 do not represent ancient empires. But if this is true, what modern nations might these beasts represent? The answer to this question is vitally important, because these nations will play a critical role as we come closer to the end of this age.

I believe that Daniel's descriptions of the beasts are veiled references to historic events in the lives of the beasts. These descriptions then become the key to understanding the identity of the beasts, and by using this key, we can uncover some surprises concerning the lion which lost its wings, the bear with three ribs in its mouth, the four-headed leopard, and the ten-horned beast that was different from the others.

In this chapter, I will attempt to prove who the four beasts of Daniel 7 are and what their importance is in these last days. However, before we examine the identity of each beast and the evidence that supports each conclusion, it might be beneficial first to take another look at Daniel 7:1–12:

In the first year of Belshazzar king of Babylon, Daniel had a dream, and visions passed through his mind as he was lying on his bed. He wrote down the substance of his dream.

Daniel said: "In my vision at night I looked, and there before me were the four great winds of heaven churning up the great sea. Four great beasts, each different from the others, came up out of the sea.

"The first was like a lion, and it had the wings of an eagle. I watched until its wings were torn off and it was lifted from the ground so that it stood on two feet as a man, and a heart of a man was given to it.

"And there before me was a second beast, which looked like a bear. It was raised up on one of its sides, and it had three ribs in its mouth between its teeth. It was told to, 'Get up and eat your fill of flesh!'

"After that, I looked and there before me was another beast, one that looked like a leopard. And on its back it had four wings like those of a bird. This beast had four heads, and it was given authority to rule.

"After that, in my vision at night I looked, and there before me was a fourth beast—terrifying and frightening and very powerful. It had large iron teeth; it crushed and devoured its victims and trampled underfoot whatever was left. It was different from all the other beasts, and it had ten horns.

"While I was thinking about the horns, there before me was another horn, a little one, which came up among them; and three of the first horns were uprooted before it. The horn had eyes like the eyes of a man and a mouth that spoke boastfully.

"As I looked,
"thrones were set in place,
and the Ancient of Days took his seat.
His clothing was white as snow;
the hair of his head was white like wool.
His throne was flaming with fire,
and its wheels were all ablaze.
A river of fire was flowing,
coming out before him.
Thousands upon thousands attended him;
ten thousand times ten thousand stood before him.
The court was seated,
and the books were opened.

"Then I continued to watch because of the boastful words the horn was speaking. I kept looking until the beast was slain and its body destroyed and thrown into the blazing fire. (The other beasts had been stripped of their authority, but were allowed to go on living for a period of time.)"

The Lion

Most commentators agree that the "great sea" spoken of in Daniel 7 does not represent the Mediterranean Sea, but rather the great mass of Gentile Humanity around the world. Assuming this to be true, the four beasts (or nations) of Daniel's vision will rise up out of the Gentile world population.

In his classic book, *The Coming Prince*, Sir Robert Anderson states that the lion could only be the British Empire. As the quote from Dr. Morris noted in the previous chapter, Scripture indicates that this could be an accurate identification.

In Daniel 7, the lion is depicted as having the wings of an eagle, which denotes its ability to soar to great heights. If any nation, or empire, ever soared to great heights, it was Great Britain. The British Empire was the largest geographical empire the world has ever known. At the height of its power and influence, it has been said that the sun never sets on the British Empire.

Just as Greek was the universal language during the first century after Christ because of Alexander the Great's world conquests, English has become the universal language in these last days because of the world conquests of the British Empire. God, in His sovereign plan, has used both languages to carry the gospel to the ends of the earth at different points in history.

On the royal coat of arms of Great Britain, the lion (which is the symbol of the country) is seen standing on its hind legs in a position known as the "rampant lion." The British lion ruled arrogantly over its vast world empire. (As you may remember, it was the arrogance of England that led to the Boston Tea Party and ultimately the revolution that cost the empire its colonies in the United States.) But then, as we read in Daniel 7:4, "[the lion's] wings were torn off." By the conclusion of World War II, the German aerial attacks had demolished London and other important English cities, and the country lay in shambles. Britain's colonies were in revolt, her industries were in disarray, and she was reduced to a second-rate power. Her wings had indeed been torn off, and she would never soar again.

Then, in Daniel's vision, he sees this beast "lifted up from the ground so that it stood on two feet like a man" (Dan. 7:4). After World War II, the Marshall Plan and the American Lend-Lease program virtually lifted Great Britain up from the rubble of its war-torn cities and put it on its feet again. However, this time England stood not as an arrogant lion ruling a global empire but as a humbled man.

Derek Prince, in his tract *Our Debt to Israel*, suggests that England lost its empire because she opposed the rebirth of Israel in 1947–48. He writes:

> From that very moment in history, Great Britain's empire underwent a process of decline and disintegration so rapid and total that it cannot be accounted merely by the relevant political, military or economic factors. Today, less than a generation later, Britain, (like Spain who cast the Jews out of their country during the 15th and 16th centuries) is a struggling second-rate power. This represents, in part at least, the outworking of a divine principle stated in Isaiah 60:12, "For the nation and kingdom that will not serve thee shall perish; yea, those nations will be utterly wasted."[1]

I believe that much of end-times prophecy centers on Israel and the nations that have dealt harshly with God's people. However, while Great Britain's opposition to the new nation of Israel may very well have been the cause of its downfall, its disintegration had ultimately already been foretold in Daniel 7:4.

Daniel then writes that "the heart of a man was given to [the lion]" (Dan. 7:4). In 1945, the British leadership began to realize that they were no longer in a position to maintain and control their worldwide empire, so they proceeded to make humanitarian gestures around the world. By the end of 1948, England had given independence or commonwealth status to forty-three nations. Never in the annals of history had a nation given away its empire, yet Great Britain, in its humbled condition as a lion with the heart of a man, did just that.[2]

Tarshish and the Lioness

Another passage of Scripture that has caused prophecy experts some disagreement in interpretation is Ezekiel 38:13, which states, "Sheba and Dedan and the merchants of Tarshish and all her villages [or strong lions] will say to you, 'Have you come to plunder? Have you gathered your hordes to loot, to carry off silver and gold, to take away livestock and goods and to seize much plunder?'"

If we accept that Great Britain is the lion of Daniel 7:4, it may be possible to discover the identity of Tarshish and her strong lions. However, in this passage, Ezekiel is prophesying against the land of Magog, which many scholars believe was the ancient land of the Sythians and is now the southern area of the former Soviet Empire. As we previously mentioned, in the last days, the Muslim nations of the old Soviet Union (and likely Russia proper), along with the Muslim nations of the Middle East, are going to charge down from the North with a huge army and invade Israel (the battle of Armageddon). The maritime nation of Tarshish, whose merchant ships dominated the Mediterranean Sea during biblical times, was thought to be located somewhere on the western coast of Spain. This ancient country sank below the sands of time long ago, so this Tarshish of Ezekiel 38:13 must refer to a future, modern-day, maritime nation that is on the scene during the last days.

History has told us that before Great Britain lost her empire, she "ruled the waves," forging an empire with her mighty navy. Britain is still dependent on its merchant marine fleet today, which seems to indicate that Great Britain could be this biblical modern-day maritime nation. Of course, if this were the only evidence available, there wouldn't be much on which to stake a claim. Fortunately, there is more.

The translators of the Septuagint (the Greek translation of the Hebrew Bible, so named because it was supposedly translated by seventy Palestinian Jewish scholars) translated the "lion" of Daniel 7 as a lioness.[3] Subsequent English translations omitted the gender of the lion of Daniel 7. This was probably done because the translators did not think the gender of the lion made a difference—after all, a lion is a lion, whether it is male or female. However, if this lion of Daniel 7:4 is seen as a lioness, a connection can be made between this beast and the modern-day maritime nation called "Tarshish."

In the *Amplified Bible,* the "villages" (or "strong lions") associated with Tarshish are translated as "lionlike cubs." The *Scofield Reference Bible* and the *Jerusalem Bible* translate "villages" as "young lions." Who but a lioness produces lion cubs? The *Living Bible* paraphrases these associates of Tarshish as "merchant princes of Tarshish with whom she trades." I believe that this is significant, because it could indicate that America is one of Tarshish's lion cubs.

One of the primary questions people ask in a discussion of biblical prophecy is: where is America depicted in end-times prophecy? Because the beasts of Daniel 7 have been misinterpreted to be ancient empires, most futurist expositors do not believe that the United States will play a role in end-times events. Others maintain that America is not seen in prophecy because the nation will go through an economic collapse and become subservient to the revived Roman Empire. However, if Tarshish and the lion represent Great Britain, then the "strong lions" could represent the strongest nations that have come out of the English lioness: New Zealand, Canada, Australia, and the United States of America.

Sheba and Dedan

But what about the identify of Sheba and Dedan? What nations do these represent in Ezekiel 38:13? From Scripture, we know that Sheba and Dedan were the grandsons of Keturah, the second wife of Abraham. According to Genesis 25:1–6, Abraham left all he had to Isaac and sent Keturah's offspring to the East.

Modern archaeological evidence places Dedan about 250 miles north of Medina and Sheba in modern Yemen. Thus, it appears that Sheba and Dedan (Saudi Arabia), along with the merchants of Tarshish (the business or government interests of Great Britain) and her "strong lions" New Zealand, Canada, Australia, and the United States ask Gog (Russia and the Islamic conferation) what their intentions are regarding the last-days invasion of Israel. I believe these "strong lion" nations may ally themselves with Saudi Arabia to protect their oil interests after the Beast signs the covenant with Israel for her protection.

Why would Saudi Arabia—a Muslim nation—have to ask this question of the Islamic confederation? We know that the Saudi royal family has historically tried to straddle two conflicting positions. On the one hand, they want to maintain their relations with the United States, where many of the Saudi royal family have been educated and where they are heavily invested. On the other hand, they want to keep the Saudi Islamists at bay by pouring money into the *jihad* (holy war) that the Islamic world considers to be an agent to spread, protect, and cleanse the Islamic faith. This is a precarious edge to walk. If the circumstances allowed, the fundamentalist Muslims could use the *jihad* to eliminate the Saudi royal family. In his book *The Last of the Giants,* George Otis, Jr., the CEO, founder, and president of The Sentinel Group, states the following about the Saudi royal family's position:

> While Mecca and Medina are administrated currently by the outwardly straitlaced Saudis, many fundamentalists view the Arabian regime as compromised and corrupt. In fact, so strongly do these elements disapprove of Saudi guardianship, that any major Jihad against the infidel Israelis will almost surely endeavor to topple the "apostate" House of the Saudi en route.[4]

Apparently, the Saudi family's concern for their own safety will be the reason they will question the leaders of the North—the majority of whom will be those of the Islamic faith—asking what their intentions are regarding the invasion of Israel. When the Islamic invaders of Israel are confronted with this question from Saudi Arabia and with the backing of the "strong lion" nations they may think twice about taking out the Saudi family.

Euroskepticism and NAFTA

Note that in Daniel 7:11–12, after the Beast is destroyed, the other beasts are "allowed to live for a period of time." This indicates that the lioness is not part of the ten-horned beast and that it will remain sovereign even after the battle of Armageddon. Because of this, I believe that Great Britain's withdrawal from the EU is imminent. (If it has not already happened by the time of this printing.)

The second Gulf War might have signaled the beginning of Great Britain's break with the EU. During this war, England sided with America against the majority of the other nations on the European continent. Recall that we mentioned previously that when a poll was taken in Britain some months before the EU's Lisbon constitution went on line, eighty-one percent of the British population expressed disfavor with the EU constitution and wanted a referendum vote on membership in the British Parliament. When Queen Elizabeth II signed the ratification of the Lisbon Treaty, the British populace was denied a voice in this vote, which only added to their dissatisfaction with the EU.

It seems that the British people have long been skeptical of the Eurocrats in Brussels. They fear that these Eurocrats, who now regulate everything in the EU, from fisheries to meat sanitation, will attempt to dominate all areas of English life. For that and other reasons, "Euroskepticism" runs high among the British people in regard to forming a closer union with the EU. The British would much prefer a loose association of nations in a free trade relationship rather than a federal Europe.

Britain has stronger financial, military, and commercial ties with the United States than it does with any country in Europe. Some time back, the nation decided to take a "watch and see" attitude when the European Monetary Fund was being formed. Because of this refusal to join the European Monetary Union, they may find themselves with no other alternative than to look across the Atlantic for economic survival.

The North American Free Trade Agreement (NAFTA) is currently a trilateral trade bloc between the United States, Canada, and Mexico. Now that we can be relatively certain that Great Britain is the lioness of Daniel 7, it follows that if the country withdraws from the EU (the ten-horned beast), it will probably join NAFTA and bring with it the Commonwealth nations of Australia and New Zealand. At this point, the trade agreement may even change its name to the "North Atlantic Free Trade Association," as Prime Minister Margaret Thatcher suggested some years ago.

In an article in the December 1997 issue of *The European*, Andrew Sullivan made the following case for Britain's application for NAFTA membership:

> The British economy is structured on American rather than European lines; low unemployment, flexible labour markets, tight money, open trade. The American-UK economic cycles are roughly aligned—and

far more than those between, say, Britain and Germany. American companies own 3,500 plants in Britain—almost four times the number of Germany's. Of course, there are Mexico and Canada to worry about. But cheap Mexican labour can only help the British consumer get cheaper products, and Canada's economy is as closely linked to the British as America's. Britain is Canada's third largest trading partner after the United States (which does not really count), and Japan. And after America, Britain is the largest foreign investor in Canada, accounting for a quarter of all foreign investments in the country.[5]

When Britain joins NAFTA and the Beast confirms the covenant to protect Israel for the seven-year period, this English-speaking trading bloc may possibly drop their support of Israel and make an alliance with Saudi Arabia in order to protect their oil interests in the Middle East.

The presence of Mexico in NAFTA poses a problem, as Ezekiel 38:13 does not give any indication of any other nations in this association other than Sheba, Dedan, Tarshish and her "strong lions." However, this dilemma might be solved by the fact that, as of the writing of this book, Mexico is on the verge of collapse. In an article in the *Las Vegas Sun,* one reporter quoted four-star general Barry McCaffrey, a drug czar under President Clinton, as saying, "the situation [in Juarez] is deteriorating so fast that Mexico is on the edge of abyss."[6] It appears to be a question of *when* Mexico will collapse, not *if.* If such were the case, Mexico's position with NAFTA would obviously be impaired or obliterated.

The Bear

The "bear" in Daniel's vision could very well represent communist Russia. In Daniel 7:5, the prophet states that the bear "was lifted up on one of its sides." Communist Russia rose up on Europe's eastern side, controlling East Berlin, East Germany, and Eastern Europe. Only the NATO allies kept the Russian bear from rising up towards the West.

Of course, an objection might be made that this is no longer the case given the demise of communism in Europe. However, we have to remember that the description of the beasts in Daniel 7 corresponds to the time the book of Daniel was unsealed in 1948. The fall of communism occurred later than 1948. This is an event known by most of the world as "Pax Europe" or the "peace of Europe." This peace is being threatened today by a phoenix-like, aggressive, totalitarian government that is rising up out of the ashes of the old communist regime.

The bear in Daniel's prophecy has three ribs locked firmly between its teeth (see Dan. 7:5). In 1939, Hitler and Stalin signed the Nazi-Soviet Pact, a secret agreement in which both countries pledged not to invade each other. The treaty also included a secret protocol for dividing Eastern Europe between the two nations. Following its signing, Germany and the Soviet Union invaded their respective portions of Poland, and the Soviets annexed the three small Baltic nations of Latvia, Lithuania, and Estonia. Later, in 1941, Hitler double-crossed Stalin, invaded Russia, and took the three nations back. However, at the conclusion of the war in 1945, the Soviets reclaimed these territories, and they became unwilling Russian satellite states caught in the jaws of the Russian bear. Russia moved in thousands of its population and military personnel in an effort to dilute regional nationalism and tighten its jaws on these three Baltic nations.

In Daniel's vision, the bear was told to "get up and eat [its] fill of flesh" (Dan. 7:5). It is common knowledge that communist Russia ruthlessly murdered untold millions of innocent people. Shallow graves are still being found where thousands were hastily buried by bulldozers. One United Press release reported, "Western estimates of Stalin's systematic slaughter range between ten to twenty million people"[7] For seventeen years—1930 to 1947—the Russian bear feasted on the flesh of innocent men, women, and children. The God of heaven has not forgotten.

The Leopard

I believe that the strange-looking leopard, with its four heads and four small bird wings, is the old colonial Indian Empire that was ruled by Great Britain for more than 250 years. This empire was composed of the four nations of Sri Lanka, Burma (Myanmar), Pakistan, and India, representing the four heads of the leopard—an animal whose home region is in southern Asia. The fact that the creature in Daniel's vision also has four birdlike wings may denote that these four nations will rise to power but never to the heights the lioness obtained with its wings of an eagle. Beyond a shadow of a doubt, this leopard does *not* represent the Greek Empire of Alexander the Great.

In the last sentence of Daniel 7:6, the prophet states that the leopard "was given authority to rule." Great Britain gave independence to all four of these nations within a short four-month period—from late 1947 to early 1948. Without ever firing a shot, these nations gained self-rule.

As of 2009, these nations had a combined population of 1,389,682,903. That comes out to be 59,638,298 *more* than the People's Republic of China.[8] Along with the advantage of having a high population from which to draw troops, at least two of these countries—India and Pakistan—now possess nuclear weapons.

Over the past few decades, India has been steadily building its military to the point where it could now be considered an Asian superpower. Brahma Chellaney, Professor of Strategic Studies at the Centre for Policy Research, states the following regarding this shift:

India has come a long way since it gained independence from British Colonial rule a little more than 40 years ago. In the West, images of India remain stereotyped. A land of poverty, snake charmers, elephants, elections violence and slums. But in reality the world's most populous democracy is quietly becoming a leading industrial and military power. India now has the world's third-largest pool of scientific manpower, just after the superpowers. It is producing scientists, engineers and doctors at a rate that far outstrips its economy's capacity to absorb them, resulting in a heavy brain drain. India has the world's fourth largest military machine after the U.S., Soviet Union and China. India has achieved not only agricultural self sufficiency but also, at the moment, a glut.[9]

In Revelation 16:12, John writes that when "the sixth angel poured out his bowl on the great river Euphrates … its water was dried up to prepare the way for the kings from the East." If these four nations represent the leopard, then they might also represent these "kings from the East" who will come against the Beast during the battle of

Armageddon. Islam is spreading rapidly in each of these four nations and could very well be the driving force that will involve them in the invasion of the last days. In his May 20, 1985 radio program, Hal Lindsey said that, according to his intelligence sources, Russia, Iran, and India have made a military alliance. If this is true (and still in effect), it could force India to join with Russia and the Islamic nations in their invasion of Israel at the battle of Armageddon.

Interestingly, the word "leopard" comes from the Greek *leopardos* (*leon*, meaning "lion" and *pardos*, meaning "male panther"). In ancient times, the animal was thought to be a hybrid of these two species. In the same way, the British lion was, and still remains, a symbolic part of the old Indian Empire. Great Britain's imprint has been indelibly left on these four nations' architectures, government structures, and customs. Note that each of the three beasts in Daniel 7:4–6 came on to the world scene in sequential order. The lion of Great Britain declined as the Russian bear came on the scene. Then the colonial Indian Empire nations (the leopard) received their independence.

The Fourth Beast

The next great power to arise was the European Union, which I believe represents the fourth beast of Daniel's vision.

As previously mentioned, the fourth beast is a representation of ancient Rome, which will develop "ten horns" in the last days (much like the legs of iron and the ten toes of Daniel 2). What we have in view here in Daniel's vision is the modern nation of the ten horns. Because the ten horns are a revival of the Roman Empire, that ancient empire is seen as the body, or root, that supports the present-day horns.

The Roman Empire, depicted as the iron legs in Daniel 2, crushed and devoured its victims and trampled underfoot whatever was left. The fact that the fourth beast has "teeth of iron" tells us that it is connected with ancient Rome, while the "nails of brass" tell us that it represents the Roman Empire of today, because the Beast, during the time of this revived Roman Empire, desecrates the Temple. The Beast's desecration of the Temple is parallel to the desecration of the Temple by Antiochus Epiphanes, who represented the Syrian fourth of the Greek (brass) Empire.

THE FOUR EMPIRES OF DANIEL 2 AND 7

A Comparison Chart of the Four empires of Daniel Chapters 2 and 7

Nebuchadnezzar's Dream—Dan. 2	Daniel's Interpretation	Daniel's vision. Ch. 8	Expositor's Assuumption	Daniel's vision—Ch.7 / Identity Change Suggested by Author
HEAD OF GOLD	Babylon		Lion (Babylon)	Lion Great Britain
CHEST AND ARMS OF SILVER	Medo-Persia	Ram Medo-Persia (Dan. 8:20)	Bear (Medo-Persia)	Bear Communist Russia
BELLY AND THIGHS OF BRONZE	Greece	Goat Greece (Dan. 8:21)	Leopard (Greece)	Leopard The Old Indian Empire*
LEGS OF IRON			Ancient Rome	
FEET OF IRON AND CLAY	Holy Roman Empire			

TOES OF IRON AND CLAY—Revived Roman Empire ——— (European Union formed from Ancient Rome.) Ten Horned Beast.

*India
Pakistan
Sri Lanka
Burma
  (Myanmar)

Summary

Most commentators agree that the "great sea" spoken of in Daniel 7 represents the great mass of Gentile Humanity around the world. Given this, the four beasts, or nations, of Daniel's vision will rise up out of the Gentile world population. I believe these four beasts are Great Britain (the lioness); communist Russia (the bear); the old colonial Indian Empire nations of India, Pakistan, Burma, and Sri Lanka (the leopard); and the EU (the ten-horned beast), which represents a revival of the ancient Roman Empire. It is important for us to identify these nations so that we can understand what will take place during the last days and know how these modern nations will affect our lives.

The first of the beasts represents the British Empire. The British Empire was the largest the world has ever known, but after World War II, its "wings were torn off" and it was given "the heart of a man" (Dan. 7:4). By the end of 1948, England had given independence to forty-three nations—an act that has never been paralleled in history.

The lioness of Daniel 7 can be connected with Tarshish and the "lion-like cubs" of Ezekiel 38:13. Britain is still dependent on its merchant marine fleet, which seems to indicate that Great Britain could be the biblical modern-day maritime nation of Tarshish. The "lion-like cubs" probably represent the nations that have come out of the lioness—such as New Zealand, Canada, Australia, and the United States.

The identity of Sheba and Dedan can also be determined. Sheba and Dedan were the grandsons of Keturah, the second wife of Abraham. They settled in the Arabian Peninsula in what is modern-day Saudi Arabia. Scripture states that in the last days, Sheba and Dedan (Saudi Arabia), along with the merchants of Tarshish (the business or government interests of Britain) and her "lion-like cubs" (former English colonies), will ask Gog (Russia and the Islamic confederation) what their intentions are regarding their invasion of Israel.

After England's withdrawal from the EU, she may join the United States and Canada in NAFTA, bringing with her the commonwealth nations of Australia and New Zealand. This association of English-speaking nations will be a refuge for those who are fortunate enough to escape a new "iron curtain of Europe" erected by the Beast during the period that we call the persecution, which will begin in the middle of the seven years.

The bear, the second beast, represents communist Russia. As Daniel 7:5 states, it was "lifted up on one of its sides" (controlled Eastern Europe), had "three ribs in its mouth between its teeth" (annexed Latvia, Lithuania, and Estonia), and ate its "fill of flesh" (murdered untold millions of people).

The third beast, the four-headed leopard represents the old colonial Indian Empire ruled by Great Britain (modern-day Sri Lanka, Burma [Myanmar], Pakistan, and India). The leopard was given "authority to rule" when Great Britain gave independence to each of these nations in 1947–1948 (Dan. 7:6). These nations may also represent the "kings from the East" (Rev. 16:12) who will come against the Beast during the battle of Armageddon.

The fourth beast, with the ten horns, as we have already seen, represents the EU. The fact that it has "teeth of iron" connects it to ancient Rome, while the "nails of brass" connect it to the Roman Empire of today, for Scripture states the Beast will desecrate the Temple (2 Thess. 2:3–4) during the time of this revived empire just as Antiochus Epiphanes did during the time he ruled the Syrian fourth of Alexander's Greek Empire (the brass portion of the image of Daniel 2).

CHAPTER 8

MYSTERY BABYLON

As we have seen, there will not be a one-world government. But will there be a one-world church during the time of the apocalypse? The answer to this question is important, as we know that the church will be present on earth during the persecution of the Beast.

For decades, an argument has been raging regarding the Babylon (or Babylons) spoken of in Revelation 17 and 18. One side says this Babylon is both a religious harlot and a commercial center called "Mystery Babylon." The other side says there will be two Babylons, but in different locations: a religious one in Rome and a rebuilt, commercial one in Iraq.

What does Scripture say? The angel in Revelation 17 gives John a description of the woman called "Mystery Babylon" in the following verses:

> One of the seven angels who had the seven bowls came and said to me, "Come, I will show you the punishment of the great prostitute, who sits on many waters. With her the kings of the earth committed adultery and the inhabitants of the earth were intoxicated with the wine of her adulteries."

Then the angel carried me away in the Spirit into a desert. There I saw a woman sitting on a scarlet beast that was covered with blasphemous names and had seven heads and ten horns. The woman was dressed in purple and scarlet, and was glittering with gold, precious stones and pearls. She held a golden cup in her hand, filled with abominable things and the filth of her adulteries. This title was written on her forehead:

MYSTERY

BABYLON THE GREAT

THE MOTHER OF PROSTITUTES

AND THE ABOMINATIONS OF THE EARTH.

I saw that the woman was drunk with the blood of the saints, the blood of those who bore testimony to Jesus.

When I saw her, I was greatly astonished. Then the angel said to me: "Why are you astonished? I will explain to you the mystery of the woman and the beast she rides, which has the seven heads and ten horns. The beast, which you saw, once was, now is not, and will come up out of the Abyss and go to his destruction. The inhabitants of the earth whose names have not been written in the book of life from the creation of the world will be astonished when they see the beast, because he once was, now is not, and yet will come.

"This calls for a mind with wisdom. The seven heads are seven hills on which the woman sits. They are also seven kings. Five have fallen, one is, the other has not yet come; but when he does come, he must remain for a little while. The beast who once was, and now is not, is an eighth king. He belongs to the seven and is going to his destruction....

Then the angel said to me, "The waters you saw, where the prostitute sits, are peoples, multitudes, nations and languages. The beast and the ten horns you saw will hate the prostitute. They will bring her to ruin and leave her naked; they will eat her flesh and burn her with fire. For God has put it into their hearts to accomplish his purpose by agreeing to give the beast their power to rule, until God's words are fulfilled. The woman you saw is the great city that rules over the kings of the earth."

—Revelation 17:1–11; 15–18

In this chapter, we will attempt to discern the identity of "Mystery Babylon."

I personally believe there is only one Mystery Babylon, and that it is located in Rome. Also, I will attempt to answer the question of a one-world church.

The Seven Mountains

We have already discovered that one of the meanings of the seven heads is the seven world empires that have negatively impacted Israel down through the centuries. Scripture also tells us that these seven heads represent seven "hills" on which the prostitute sits. The translation of the word "hills" in verse 9, which is the word used by most modern translations, was made by modern Protestant theologians in order to make a positive identification of the woman as Papal Rome. But in fact, the word translated "hills" should actually be "mountains."

Admittedly, Rome does sit on seven hills, or knolls, but it does not sit on seven mountains. Thus, the seven mountains must be symbolic of something else other than actual mountains. Using the rule of interpretation that Scripture will interpret Scripture, we find a reference to Babylon as a mountain in Jeremiah 51:25, where the Lord says:

> I am against you, O destroying mountain, you who destroy the whole earth.... I will stretch out my hand against you, roll you off cliffs, and make you a burned-out mountain.

Babylon was located on a plain, so we know the Lord was not referring to a literal mountain in this passage.

We see another example of a symbolic mountain when Daniel, concluding the explanation of Nebuchadnezzar's dream, says to the king:

> Then the iron, the clay, the bronze, the silver and the gold were broken to pieces at the same time and became like chaff on a threshing floor in the summer. The wind swept them away without leaving a trace. But the rock that struck the statue became a huge mountain and filled the whole earth.
> —Daniel 2:35

In this verse, the symbolic mountain represents the kingdom of God, which will cover the whole earth when Jesus sets up His millennial kingdom.

From this, we see that Scripture seems to indicate that a mountain can represent an empire or a kingdom. Based on this interpretation, I suggest that the seven mountains in Revelation 17 are the same seven world empires that we have spoken of earlier: Egypt, Assyria, Babylon, Medo-Persia, Greece, Rome, and the revived Roman Empire. These have been controlled by Satan (the scarlet beast) and have negatively impacted Israel throughout history.

Notice that not only does the harlot sit on seven mountains, which represent the seven world empires, but also she rides the scarlet beast. This shows us that the harlot's religious system has influenced these seven world empires and has been carried by Satan's world system throughout the centuries. Note that she does not have any reins in her hands, which indicates that she does not have any control over the scarlet beast. The harlot has both been carried by and been dependent upon Satan's world system ever since her conception in Nimrod's Babylon after the flood.

The Origin of Mystery Babylon

I believe that Mystery Babylon, Mother of Prostitutes, represents the Roman Catholic Church in Vatican City. One reason I believe the Roman Catholic Church is called the "Mother of Prostitutes" is because she has spawned churches around the world that have incorporated many of the animistic and pagan practices of the indigenous peoples. A good example of this syncretism is found in the Caribbean and in South America where these pagan beliefs have worked their way into the rituals of the Roman Catholic churches.

True Christianity is exclusive from all other religions, and God will not share His glory with any other. As you will recall, pagan synthesis was the reason that God ejected the Israelites of the Old Testament out of the Promised Land. There is no other name given under heaven by which we must be saved other than that of Jesus (Acts 4:12). The relationship between spiritual prostitution and the Roman Catholic Church goes all the way back to Babylon, with the beginning of the first apostasy and the start of false religion. The elements of this mystical Babylonian religion originated with the worship of Nimrod's wife, Semiramis, who became known as "the Queen of Heaven." Ham was one of the three sons of Noah. Ham was the father of Cush, and Cush was the father of Nimrod. Nimrod was a leader in Babylon. Some think he was the historical Sargon I ruler of Akkad. It appears that he led the people into apostasy by constructing great towers called ziggurats, where people began to worship the sun, moon, and stars. Later, he built the city of Nineveh in Assyria. At the same time Semiramis was busy conjuring up a false mother/son religion. This was all done while Shem, the youngest son of Noah and a witness to the reality of the true God, was still alive (Gen. 10:6–12).

Semiramis claimed that, as a virgin, she had conceived a son, whom she named Tammuz. Sometime later Tammuz supposedly died, and Semiramis claimed that he had been resurrected. His resurrection was celebrated as a springtime rebirth of nature and incorporated sex orgies.

A priesthood was organized within this occult system, which claimed to have mystical secrets. This priesthood was ruled over by a high priest who had the title of "pontiff." Membership was open to all in this occult brotherhood; the only prerequisite was that the person had to relinquish his or her national identity and swear allegiance to the pontiff.

False Religion Enters the Church

When God confused the languages at Babylon, the people who were scattered carried this sexually-oriented mother/son religion to the uttermost parts of the world. It has been a part of Satan's world system throughout the ages and has been a foe of Israel as much as, if not more than, the domination of the seven world empires. During Jeremiah's time, he condemned the tribe of Judah for their participation in the worship of the Queen of Heaven (see Jer. 7:18). Later, the Jews who fled to Egypt to avoid captivity told Jeremiah that they would continue to worship the Queen of Heaven as did those before them (see Jer. 44:17, 19, 25).

The city of Babylon was Satan's stronghold until he moved his capital to Pergamos in Asia Minor, where it was during John's time (see Rev. 2:12–13). The city of Lydia in the region of Pergamos was the home of the Etruscans, who practiced this Babylonian religion and brought it with them when they settled in Italy sometime after 800 B.C. The pontiff of this occult religion became very powerful, and he was later accepted by the Romans as their civil leader. It wasn't long before the Etruscans made Julius Caesar the Supreme Pontiff in 63 B.C. In this way, the first Roman emperor became the head of the Babylonian priesthood.

The title "Supreme Pontiff" was passed on to each succeeding emperor until 376 A.D., when Damascus, the presiding bishop of the Christian church at Rome, compromised and took up the title. (Two years earlier, the Roman emperor Gratian, a Christian, had refused the title on the grounds that he didn't want anything to do with this Babylonian abomination.) Without missing a beat, Damascus assumed the title and quietly swept the occult's sexual practices under the proverbial rug. This seemingly insignificant event enabled Satan, with only a few minor changes, to synthesize the Roman Catholic Church and this Babylonian mother/son religion into one system.

This false religion, under the guise of Christianity, will continue to ride Satan's world system until the middle of the seven years, when Satan will incarnate himself in the Beast of Revelation 13. The Beast will then drop his pretense of following this false religion and dictate that those who practice it must worship him instead. The Roman Catholic Church will refuse and will be destroyed by fire (Rev. 17:16). At this point, as we have seen, the Beast will invade Israel and force his way into the Temple at Jerusalem, where he will unabashedly demand worship as Emperor God (2 Thess. 2:3–4).

In the Name of Christianity

Throughout the ages, the Roman Catholic Church has been as much a political organization as it has been an ecclesiastical one. As an ecclesiastical organization, it has been "drunk with the blood of the saints, the blood of those who bore testimony of Jesus" (Rev. 17:6). It is a widely known historical fact that during the time of the Inquisition instigated by the Roman Catholic Church, thousands of Protestants and Jews lost their lives. As a political organization, the Roman Catholic Church has served as the "great city that rules over the kings of the earth" (Rev. 17:18). Under the name of the Holy Roman Empire, the Vatican literally reigned over the kings of the earth, and she still "reigns" over many nations today. Based on this, again I say, I do not believe there are two Babylons. Rather, I believe these verses refer to the same Babylon—the church in Rome that is both religious and political/commercial.

Now if you are of the Roman Catholic faith, please understand that what I am addressing here is the institution and not the thousands of souls who are members of that institution. I believe there are born-again believers in the Roman Catholic Church who have decided to remain in that institution for one reason or another. However, I also believe that they have been born again by the work of the Holy Spirit, and not because they are members of the Roman Catholic Church.

In Ephesians 2:8–10 Paul says:

> For by grace have you been saved, through faith—and this not of yourselves, it is a gift of God—not by works, so that no one can boast. For we are God's workmanship, created in Christ Jesus to do good works, which God prepared in advance for us to do.

The only means by which we can receive salvation is through God's unmerited favor and faith that Jesus died for our sins. Our works have nothing to do with our salvation; they are simply an expression of our love for the One who has saved us. If we could earn points with God toward salvation by the things we do, then Christ's blood on the cross would have been meaningless.

Prophecy Unfulfilled?

As we mentioned at the beginning of this chapter, there are some who believe that the angel who gave John the vision in Revelation 17 was referring to two separate Babylons: a religious organization in Rome and a rebuilt, commercial center in Iraq. However, if this were true, there would be no reason for the angel to call Babylon a "mystery." A mystery implies that something has been hidden or kept secret. On the other hand, if Mystery Babylon represents a false religion *and* a political/commercial center in one location, then we do have a mystery.

Let's look at some interesting similarities between what Jeremiah says about ancient Babylon and what Revelation says about modern-day Mystery Babylon. In Jeremiah 51:6–8, the prophet writes:

> Flee from Babylon! Run for your lives! Do not be destroyed because of her sins. It is time for the LORD's vengeance; he will repay her what she deserves. Babylon was a gold cup in the LORD's hand; she made the whole earth drunk. The nations drank her wine; therefore they have now gone mad. Babylon will suddenly fall and be broken.

What Jeremiah says about ancient Babylon is very similar to what the angel says to John about Mystery Babylon in Revelation 18:

> All the nations have drunk the maddening wine of her adulteries…. "Come out of her, my people, so that you will not share her sins…." Therefore in one day her plagues will overtake her: death, mourning and famine. She will be consumed by fire.
>
> —Revelation 18:3–4, 8

Babylon has not yet been destroyed to the extent of Jeremiah's prophecy. We know this because in Jeremiah 51:25–26, the Lord, speaking about the judgment coming to Babylon, says, "I will stretch out my hand against you, roll you off cliffs, and make you a burned-out mountain. No rock will be taken from you for a cornerstone, nor any stone for a foundation, for you will be desolate forever." Travelers to Iraq report that many cities in the country have used bricks from ancient Babylon for building purposes. Therefore, biblical Babylon has not yet been completely broken, and the prophecies against it have not yet been fulfilled.

I would like to suggest that perhaps the reason the prophecies regarding the destruction of ancient Babylon have not yet been fulfilled is because they will be fulfilled in the destruction of Papal Rome, the modern-day Mystery Babylon.

Those who support the theory of the two Babylons maintain that it is the ecclesiastical organization in Rome that is seen being destroyed by the Beast and the ten horns in Revelation 17, whereas it is the political/ commercial city in Iraq that is destroyed by God in Revelation 18. However, by comparing the two passages of Scripture, we see that it is God who judges the Babylons in Revelation 17 and 18 by fire:

> They [the Beast and the ten horns] will bring her to ruin and leave her naked; they will eat her flesh and *burn her with fire*. For God has put it into their hearts to *accomplish his purpose* by agreeing to give the beast their power to rule, until God's words are fulfilled.
> —Revelation 17:16–17, emphasis mine

> *She will be consumed by fire*, for mighty is the Lord God who judges her.
> —Revelation 18:8, emphasis mine

The ten horns are instruments in the hands of God. All the Old Testament prophecies spoken against Babylon will be fulfilled with the destruction of the mystical Babylonian religion and the political/ commercial Babylon in Rome. Because the prostitute church refuses to worship the Beast, the Vatican State, along with the city of Rome, will be burned to the ground by the Beast and the nations of the EU (Rev. 17:16–18, 18:2–24).

The Kings

In Revelation 18:9, a voice from heaven says to John, "When the kings of the earth who committed adultery with her [Mystery Babylon] and shared her luxury see the smoke of her burning, they will weep and mourn over her." Who are these "kings" who will mourn over the loss of Rome? We know that the Beast and the EU, which includes the "ten kings," will burn and consume the city of Rome (see Rev. 17:16–17). However, there are other "kings" who have benefitted from the financial and commercial aspects of Rome along with the nations of the EU. When they see this destruction, they will be appalled and mourn their losses (Rev. 17:9–10).

In the biblical sense spiritual adultery is covetousness (lusting for the things of this world, rather than God, thus breaking the first, second, seventh and tenth commandments (see Exodus 20:3–17). These kings who share in Babylon's luxuries will mourn for the material things they have lost—items they desired more than a relationship with the God of the Universe. They will be "terrified at her torment, they will stand far off and cry: 'Woe! Woe, O great city, O Babylon, city of power!'" (Rev. 18:10).

As a side note, in Revelation 18:18 John writes, "Every sea captain, and all who travel by ship, the sailors, and all who earn their living from the sea, will stand far off. When they see the smoke of her burning, they will exclaim, 'Was there ever a city like this great city'" (Rev. 18:18)? If the Babylon referred to in this passage were in Iraq and the seafaring men were watching from the Persian Gulf, they would not be able see the smoke of the fire, because Babylon is approximately 300 miles inland from the Gulf. However, they would be able to see the smoke of the fires rising from the Vatican and Rome from the Tyrrhenian Sea. This is yet another indication that the Babylon in Revelation 18:10 refers to Rome.

A New Babylon

When John first receives the vision of the woman in Revelation 17:3, she is riding on the back of a satanic beast. The fact that this prostitute is riding on the back of Satan's world system indicates that we are dealing with one entity engaged in two separate blasphemies. On the one hand, she is participating in false religion; on the other hand, she is pursuing worldly political and commercial interests. This woman seems to enjoy riding this worldly system with all its blasphemous names while at the same time prostituting spiritual matters.

Those who stand by the two-Babylons theory believe that after the Beast destroys Rome, he will build a new Babylon as his capital in Iraq. This idea was seen as more of a possibility after Saddam Hussein rebuilt replicas of a few of the ancient buildings at the site of Old Babylon, but it still has flaws. As we discussed, after the Beast destroys Rome during the middle of the seven years, he will move against Israel and set himself up as God in the Temple in Jerusalem, where he will remain until the battle of Armageddon (Dan. 11:44–45). It seems illogical that the Beast would build a new Babylon as the capital of his empire, since he couldn't begin construction on it until the middle of the seven years, when he becomes supernatural and demands worship as Emperor God. There simply wouldn't be enough time for him to build a new city the size, scale, and scope of the one given in Scripture and have it fully operational before the battle of Armageddon.

In addition, because the Beast will have already set himself up as God in Jerusalem, he will have no need of another "capital" in Iraq. There is no Scriptural proof that verifies his capital will be anywhere else other than Jerusalem (Dan. 11:45, 2 Thess. 2:3–4).

Proof Positive

I believe that there is persuasive evidence for a political/commercial Babylon being destroyed along with a religious Babylon, and that they are one and the same. This evidence is found in Revelation 18:4: "Then I heard another voice from heaven say, 'Come out of her my people, so that you will not share in her sins, so that you will not receive any of her plagues.'"

Will there be any of God's people in an Islamic-dominated Babylon after the rapture and at the end of the seven years? I don't think so, as they would have been taken out by the rapture, killed by the Beast, or killed by Muslims. On the other hand, if the Vatican in Rome is both the religious and political/commercial Babylon (and is destroyed before the pre-wrath rapture), there may be a great many of God's people there at that time. The angel's warning would have real motivation and meaning for those who are saved.

No Super World Church

The Roman Catholic Church, or any other religious system, will never become a one-world church for the simple reason that there won't be a one-world government to enforce, or enable, a false religious system to become such a one-world church. Another reason is the fact that the *believing church* of Jesus will still be here on earth during the persecution of the Beast and will remain on earth until the day the wrath of God falls. This *believing church* will not compromise with the Beast, which will effectively prevent a worldwide religious system from becoming a reality.

Because Islamic doctrine is anti-Western, the idea of a one-world church appears to be unworkable. The Saudis, in particular, suppress anything that seems even vaguely Christian in their country.

A political cartoon appeared in The Sonora Democrat, a local California newspaper illustrating this fact during the Christmas season. The cartoon showed three robed figures holding the reins of their camels as they stood in front of a small shack with the Bethlehem star shining brightly overhead. Responding to an obvious inquiry from inside as to whether or not they might be the three wise men, they replied, "No … we're from Saudi Arabia. We just wanted to make sure there's nothing going on here that might offend us"

Now it is true that the Roman Catholic Church could try to use the fact that both they and the practitioners of Islam are descended from the same mother/son religion (which still echoes within the belief system of Middle Eastern peoples today) to try to lure Muslims to join them in a world church. However, this effort would not be successful because of Islamic antagonism toward the Western world. Muslims would never entertain the idea of joining forces with the Western Roman Catholic Church, and they would certainly never worship a Western leader. They would choose death first.

The Arab world still remembers the wars waged against them during the Crusades—wars that were carried out in the name of Christianity by the Roman Catholic Church. Furthermore, the West, with its consumerism and secularism, is seen as a threat against Islam because it seeks to change traditional Muslim ways. Because of this, and because the West supports the nation of Israel, the Koran justifies Muslims in waging a holy war (or *jihad*) against those in Western nations. Whenever Islam is threatened (or even imagined to be threatened), this continuing holy war is inflamed.

In Islamic ideology, all Muslims are considered to be in the "House of God," while those in the West (non Muslims) are said to be in the "House of War." Because of this, the Islamists must continue the war until the entire West has been converted to Islam either by voluntary submission or by the sword.

The "Uprooted" Horns

Before ending this discussion on Mystery Babylon, I would like to interject one final theory about the possible identification of the three "uprooted" horns of Daniel 7:8 and why the "little horn" (the Beast) uproots them. In Daniel 7:8 we read the following:

> While I was thinking about the horns, there before me was another horn, a little one, which came up among them; and three of the first horns were uprooted before it. This horn had eyes like the eyes of a man and a mouth that spoke boastfully.

It is my conviction that the little horn will come up from among the ten horns during the middle of the seven years. It is at the middle of the seven years that Delors will be indwelt by Satan and becomes supernatural. This is what is meant by the little horn "coming up among them (the ten horns). This is based on the fact that in this passage the Beast is called the "little horn," which suggests that he has already been given power and authority by the EU. We know from Revelation 17:13 that this power and authority have been given willingly by the ten horns (and the other nations of the EU). This indicates that the uprooting must take place sometime after the events of Revelation 17:13, and after Delors has been indwelt by Satan.

Daniel 7:8 says the Beast uproots three of the *first* horns. These first horns represent three of the ten nations of the EU who entered the Single Market on December 31, 1992 without opt-outs to the Maastricht Treaty. Since we know that one of the first things the Beast will do after becoming supernaturally indwelt by Satan is destroy Rome and the Vatican State, one of these three first horns must represent Italy. The question then becomes: what other two horns will the Beast uproot at this time, and why?

One possible scenario is that the destruction of the Roman Catholic Church will provoke two nations from the original ten countries—who do not yet realize the crushing power the Beast has acquired from Satan—to rebel against him. But which two nations? It would have to be two nations for which the Roman Catholic Church represents something very meaningful in order to provoke them to rebel against the military might of the EU.

Could these two horns be Spain and Portugal? These two countries have been closely connected to the Roman Church for centuries. As you may remember, it was Spain and Portugal who carried out the instrument of torture and death called the Inquisition. The sole purpose of the Inquisition was to protect the Roman Catholic Church.

Summary

In Revelation 17:9, the angel tells John that "the seven heads are seven hills on which the woman [Mystery Babylon] sits." These "hills," which should actually be translated "mountains," are symbolic of the seven world empires of Egypt, Assyria, Babylon, Medo-Persia, Greece, Rome, and the revived Roman Empire. The harlot rides the scarlet beast, which indicates that her religious system has influenced these seven world empires and has been carried by Satan's world system throughout the centuries.

Mystery Babylon represents the Roman Catholic Church. The relationship between spiritual prostitution and the Roman Catholic Church goes all the way back to Babylon and the beginning of the first false religion. This false mother/son religion, begun by Nimrod's wife Semiramis, was carried into Rome from the region of Pergamos in Asia Minor by the Etruscans. Julius Caesar became the head of this Babylonian religion in 63 B.C., and the title of "Supreme Pontiff" was bestowed on him and each succeeding emperor (save one) until 376 A.D., when the bishop of Rome assumed the title.

Although some believe that the "Babylon" to which the angel refers in Revelation 17 represents two separate systems—a religious organization in Rome and a rebuilt commercial center in Iraq—these two are actually one and the same—the church in Rome that is both religious and political/commercial.

The judgments of God spoken by Jeremiah against Babylon have been delayed in order to complete the destruction of the ancient Babylonian mystery religion. This fulfillment will occur with the destruction of Mystery Babylon (Papal Rome) during the time of the Beast.

The Roman Catholic Church will never incorporate all the religions of the world into one worldwide system. There are three reasons for this: 1) The *believing church* of Jesus will still be on earth at the time of the persecution. (2) The Beast will not rule the world, and a one-world church cannot exist without a one-world government to enforce it. (3) No matter how far the Roman Catholic Church would be willing to yield in compromising its doctrine, Muslims would still never accept it because they identify the church with the hated West. Practitioners of Islam would never entertain the idea of joining forces with the Western Roman Church and would never worship a Western leader. They would choose death first.

CHAPTER 9

AN OVERVIEW OF THE APOCALYPSE

It's easy to get lost in unfamiliar territory without a road map. This chapter is designed to be a road map for the material already discussed in this book. Along the way, we'll pick up some tangential issues that may not be directly related to our discussion of the Apocalypse but are related to other end-times events.

History Past

The ten northern tribes of Israel were taken into captivity by the Assyrians in 722 B.C. The two southern tribes that comprised the kingdom of Judah survived for another 130 years, until they were taken into captivity by Nebuchadnezzar, king of Babylon, in 586 B.C. This was the beginning of "the times of the Gentiles." The reason the captivity of the ten northern tribes is not credited as the beginning of the times of the Gentiles is because the Temple of God was in Jerusalem, which was in the land of Judah. The Temple represented God's presence with all Israel, and its destruction in 586 B.C. was God's sign to all twelve tribes of Israel that they were entering into a prolonged time of Gentile domination and being without His blessing. The times of the

Gentiles would arch over the five kingdoms, or empires, of Babylon, Medo-Persia, Greece, Rome, and a revival of the Roman Empire called the "ten horns."

The Jews were not a sovereign nation again until 1948. Just as God had said, they were scattered throughout the world because they failed to love and obey Him after His loving kindness and tender mercies had brought them out of Egypt and settled them in the land of Israel (Deut. 28:64). The birth of the sovereign nation of Israel on May 14, 1948 was a sign that the world was entering into the "time of the end" spoken of by the prophet Daniel in Daniel 12:9, and that the time of the Gentiles would be coming to an end in the not too distant future (see Luke 21:24).

In Daniel 12:4, the angel told Daniel to seal off the words of this prophecy until "the time of the end." The unsealing occurred in 1948, with the birth of the sovereign nation of Israel. With this, the three beasts in Daniel 7 could now be identified as Great Britain (the lion), communist Russia (the bear), and the old colonial Indian Empire (the leopard). It wasn't until 1950, with the signing of the Treaty of Paris, that the fourth beast (the ten-horned beast) of Daniel 7 began to emerge out of war-torn Europe. It eventually became identified as the EU.

On December 31, 1992, the prophecy in Revelation 17:12 was fulfilled with the birth of the European Single Market. Later, the prophecy in Revelation 17:13 will be fulfilled when the Beast is appointed as the first president of a politically unified European Union.

Great Britain, thought to be the lioness of Daniel 7, is not part of the ten horns. It is my conviction that since the Lisbon Treaty (the constitution of the EU) has been enacted, England will withdraw from the EU in the near future. The EU has mandated that all twenty-seven nations have to ratify the treaty in order for it to be valid. Great Britain's withdrawal will not negate the constitution that is now on line. After Great Britain withdraws, it may join Canada and the United States in NAFTA, and if so, it will bring into this agreement the countries of Australia and New Zealand. This act would fulfill the prophecy of Ezekiel 38:13, where Saudi Arabia (Sheba and Dedan), fearful for its safety and backed by the NAFTA bloc (the merchants of Tarshish), will ask Russia (Magog) and her Islamic allies, who are gathering for an invasion of Israel at the battle of Armageddon, "Have you come to plunder? Have you gathered your hordes to loot, to carry off silver and gold, to take away livestock and goods and to seize much plunder?"

We see no countries involved in this trading bloc other than those already mentioned. Mexico, which is not one of the lioness' cubs, may not be a member of the NAFTA treaty. There are forces at work as of the writing of this book that indicate future problems inside and outside of Mexico may force that nation to be removed as a member of NAFTA.

Daniel's Seventy "Sevens"

One of the most important prophecies regarding the end times is Daniel 9:24–27. This prophecy is important because it provides an outline for God's plan for the end times in relation to Israel and the time limits for that plan. This prophecy foretells the end of the period of time that Israel will be under the punishment of God and of the end of the Messiah's first advent (Dan 9:26).

> Seventy "sevens" are decreed for your people and your holy city to finish transgression, and put an end to sin, to atone for wickedness, to bring in everlasting righteousness, to seal up vision and prophecy and to anoint the most holy. Know and understand this: From the issuing of the decree to restore and rebuild Jerusalem until the Anointed One, the ruler, comes, there will be seven "sevens", and sixty-two "sevens." It will be built with streets and a trench, but in times of trouble. After the sixty-two "sevens," the Anointed One will be cut off and will have nothing. The people of the ruler who will come will destroy the city and the sanctuary. The end will come like a flood: War will continue until the end, and desolations have been decreed. He will confirm a covenant with many for one "seven." In the middle of the "seven" he will put an end to sacrifice and offerings. And on a wing of the Temple he will set up an abomination that causes desolation, until the end that is decreed is poured out on him.

The "he" who confirms a covenant with many is the Beast. Each "seven" in this verse stands for seven "prophetic years" (a prophetic year consists of 360 days). God had ordained seventy "sevens," or 490 prophetic years (70 x 7), to be a time of punishment for the Jews. The reason for this punishment occurred when God brought the Israelites into the Promised Land. He told them that they were to allow the land to rest every seventh year (see Lev. 25:4). They did not obey this command, so God decreed 490 years of punishment on them—one year for every seventh year of disobedience.

The seventy "sevens" (490 years) are divided into three time periods. The first period of forty-nine years opened with the command by Artaxerxes to restore and rebuild Jerusalem. The second period of 434 years immediately followed and extended from the time Jerusalem was rebuilt under Nehemiah until Jesus, "the Anointed One," came. The third period of seven years will begin when the Beast makes a covenant with Israel for seven years (Dan. 9:27). At the end of these last seven years, Christ will put an end to the Gentile world system and set up His thousand-year reign on earth.

The Gap

Sir Robert Anderson, in his book *The Coming Prince*, computed the days between the time King Artaxerxes issued the decree to restore and rebuild Jerusalem to the time Jesus, the Anointed One, would come. Beginning with the date that Artaxerxes issued the decree, March 14, 445 B.C., Anderson multiplied the next sixty-nine "sevens" and came up with 483 years. Then he multiplied 483 years by 360, the number of days in the prophetic year. This equaled 173,880 days. To convert this into the Roman calendar, Anderson changed the days from a 360-day year to a 365-day year and then added 116 leap years. Being careful not to count the year 1 B.C. and 1 A.D. twice, he came up with a date of April 6, 32 A.D. This was the very day Jesus entered into Jerusalem on the back of a colt of a donkey to offer Himself to the Jewish nation as their Messiah-King. Had the Jews accepted Him at that time, the Kingdom Age would have been ushered in. However, Jesus knew this would not happen, because it was His Father's will that He die for the sins of the world. Six days later, Jesus was "cut off," or crucified. These events took place just as Daniel predicted approximately 500 years earlier (Dan. 9:24–26).

Between the sixty-ninth "seven" and the seventieth "seven,"a time gap has been in place. This "gap" is called "the Church Age." The Church Age started on the Day of Pentecost after the resurrection of Jesus and will continue until the rapture. An unanswered question is: Did the prophetic clock stop at Christ's crucifixion causing a "gap" between the sixty-ninth seven and the seventh "seven," merely to accommodate the "Church Age," or was there something running parallel with the Church Age that has a certain time limit imposed on it? I believe this may be the case. In Leviticus 26:18–29, God told the Israelites that if they didn't obey Him, and let the land enjoy its Sabbath rests (one year out of every seven) He would remove them from the Promised Land and multiply their punishment seven times over. God repeated this four times in the same chapter. This was a warning of great magnitude. Scripture confirms they continued to disobey God, so He removed them from the land and multiplied their punishment. God said during this time He would break down their stubborn pride. How long does the punishment last before their pride is broken? In chapter 11 Daniel receives the outline of the last three and one-half years of the last seven years before Christ's return. In Daniel 12:6 in answer to the question of, "How long will it be before these astonishing things are fulfilled?" The angel speaking to Daniel answered, "It will be for a time, times and a half time [three and one-half years]. When the power of the holy people has been finally broken, all these things will be completed" (Dan. 12:7).

The Gospel of the Kingdom

During the last three and one-half years of the last seven-year period, the gospel of the kingdom, as well as the gospel of grace will be proclaimed, that is, until the rapture takes place. Jesus said in Matthew 24:14 that the "gospel of the kingdom will be preached in the whole world as a testimony to the nations, and then the end will come."

This gospel of the kingdom is the same gospel that John the Baptist, Jesus, and His disciples preached while He was on earth: "Repent, for the kingdom of heaven is near" (Matt. 4:17). There are two main components to the message of the gospel of the kingdom: 1) repentance and 2) an acknowledgment that Jesus is the Messiah.

For the Jews, accepting Jesus as the Messiah means admitting He is God's Son, and in doing so, they will also acknowledge Him as David's heir and King of this kingdom. By believing this, the Jews will realize that God is going to fulfill the Davidic Covenant of 2 Samuel 7:16 through Jesus the Messiah.

The Third Temple

The Temple in Jerusalem will be rebuilt during the last seven years. Although some believe that the Mosque of the Dome of the Rock must be destroyed for this to occur, there is actually enough room for both structures on the Temple Mount. The likely site would be south of the mosque, where recent research seems to indicate Solomon's Temple once stood. (The Holy of Holies supposedly lies beneath the little Dome of the Wind, which sits on the south end of the Temple Mount.)

Of course, persuading an orthodox Jew to worship at the Temple when it shares the Mount with a heathen building would present a bit of a problem. However, orthodox Jews may be forced to compromise in order to fulfill their agenda of separating cultural Jews from religious Jews. In the mind of a religious Jew, a cultural Jew is not a Jew at all. Only those who worship at the Temple would be considered Jews, and all the rest—even though Jewish by birth—would be seen as second-class Jews, if Jews at all.

In Revelation 11:1–2, John is told: "Go and measure the Temple of God and the altar, and count the worshipers there. But exclude the outer court, do not measure it because it has been given to the Gentiles. They will trample on the holy city 42 months." Even though John is told to measure the persecution Temple, the dimensions are never given as they are in Ezekiel 40–44 with the millennial Temple. The reason for this is because Revelation 11:1–2 is not meant to give us a description of the Temple but to tell us the length of time the Gentiles will trample the Temple and Jerusalem.

However, this does tell us that the Jews will worship at the Temple with Gentiles in the outer court. It also seems to indicate that the Mosque will remain alongside the rebuilt Temple and that the orthodox Jews will make some kind of compromise. The one thing we can be sure of is that the Temple will be built on the Temple Mount before the middle of the seven years, when the Beast will enter it to set himself up as Emperor God.

According to The Temple Institute, many of the articles used in Temple worship in ancient times have been reconstructed in anticipation of a rebuilt third Temple. For example, the high priest's breastplate and gold headpiece are ready for use. The Institute is still looking for a red heifer in order to fulfill the requirements of Numbers 19:1–22. They acquired two—one in 1997 and another in 2007—that were originally declared to be kosher but were later rejected by the Institute as unsuitable. The Institute is presently also looking at ancient structural plans for building the third Temple. They are convinced the day is coming soon when they will once again be able to worship God on the Temple Mount (Temple Institute dot com). This ability to rebuild the Temple may be part of the deal for peace in the Middle East.

Peace and Safety

Jacques Delors, the Beast, has not come to power with a plan for world peace as some prophecy buffs expected he would. He will, however, bring peace to the Middle East when he confirms the covenant with Israel for seven years. The worldwide war against terrorism will still be going on when he confirms the covenant.

After the covenant is confirmed with Israel, it is possible that the nations of NAFTA (which at this point will be comprised of America, Britain, Australia, New Zealand, and Canada) will no longer feel the need to support Israel, because the EU will have taken over that job. The nations of NAFTA may then turn to protecting Saudi Arabia in order to protect their Middle-Eastern oil supply (Ezek. 38:13).

After Delors confirms the covenant(Dan. 9:27), Israel will enjoy peace until the middle of the seven years (Rev. 13:5, Dan. 9:27). Up until that time, Delors will have no reason to break the covenant, as the peace it will bring will enable him to secure his position in Europe. The Council of Ministers will appoint him for a second term, because his first term of only two and one-half years will terminate before the middle of the seven years. During this time in office, he will be building his power base.

A pamphlet put out by Greater European Missions states, "Everyone who seriously wants to commit his life to reach Europe for Christ must clearly see Europe's extremely secularized and materialistic attitude." The pamphlet goes on to say that Europe is more of a mission field than Africa or Asia and "the difference is that the European thinks that throughout the history of the Continent, Christianity has been tried, and has come to the conclusion that it didn't help." The majority of Europeans are non-practicing Roman Catholics, and materialism reigns in their hearts. All of this will play into the EU president's hands when he uses the Roman Catholic Church for his own purposes and then later destroys it (Rev. 17:3, Rev. 17:16–18).

It is probable the Pope will crown the Beast as Emperor of the Holy Roman Empire. The Pope will do this in an attempt to restore the power and prestige of the Roman Catholic Church that was lost during Napoleon's reign. Once the Beast is crowned Emperor, he will begin to change the government of the EU from a socialistic democracy to the Roman imperial form of government (which will include emperor worship—2 Thess. 2:3–4).

A Supernatural Shift

During the first three and one-half years of the seven-year period, nothing that occurs is supernatural. However, during the last three and one-half years, almost everything that takes place is supernatural. This supernatural shift begins when the Beast is indwelt by Satan at the middle of the seven years and demands worship as Emperor God. He will attempt to destroy everyone and every institution within his empire that refuses to recognize him as Emperor God.

Mystery Babylon (the apostate Roman Catholic Church) will resist worshiping the Beast. In turn, the Beast will destroy the Roman Catholic Church by fire. This burning of Rome may cause Spain and Portugal to rebel against the Beast in order to avenge the Roman Catholic Church's destruction. As a result, Portugal and Spain may be "uprooted" by the armies of the European nations under the direction of the Beast.

After uprooting the three horns (see Dan. 7:8), the Beast will engage Egypt in battle and strip the nation of all its hidden treasures.

Sudan and Libya, having common borders with Egypt, will surrender to the Beast in hopes of avoiding a similar fate.

> At the time of the end the king of the South will engage him in battle, and the king of the North will storm out against him with chariots and cavalry and a great fleet of ships. He will invade many countries and sweep though them like a flood. He will also invade the Beautiful Land. Many countries will fall, but Edom, Moab and the leaders of Ammon will be delivered from his hand. He will extend his power over many countries; Egypt will not escape. He will gain control over the treasures of gold and silver and all the riches of Egypt, with the Libyans and Nubians in submission.
>
> —Daniel 11:40–43

After sacking Egypt and taking her out of the picture, the Beast will break his covenant of protection with Israel and invade "the Beautiful Land." He will set up his throne in the Holy of Holies and demand worship as Emperor God (see Dan. 11:41; 2 Thess. 2:3–4). The Sudanese (the Nubians) and the Libyans will be able to avoid being overthrown by submitting to the demands of the Beast, and later they will join Russia and the Islamic forces against the Beast in the battle of Armageddon (see Ezek. 38:5).

In addition to the supernatural events happening with the Beast, sometime during the first part of the last three and one-half years, an angel will be seen flying in mid-air proclaiming the eternal gospel to the world. Two more angels will follow him. The second angel will announce the destruction of Babylon (Rome), while the third angel will warn people not to take the mark of the Beast:

> Then I saw another angel flying in midair, and he had the eternal gospel to proclaim to those who live on the earth—to every nation, tribe, language and people. He said in a loud voice, "Fear God and give him glory, because the hour of his judgment has come. Worship him who made the heavens, the earth, the sea and the springs of water."
>
> A second angel followed and said, "Fallen! Fallen is Babylon the Great, which made all nations drink the maddening wine of her adulteries."

A third angel followed them and said in a loud voice: "If anyone worships the beast and his image and receives his mark on his forehead or on his hand, he, too, will drink the wine of God's fury, which has been poured full strength into the cup of his wrath. He will be tormented with burning sulfur in the presence of the holy angels and the Lamb. And the smoke of their torment rises forever and ever. There is no rest day or night for those who worship the beast and his image, or for anyone who receives the mark of his name." This calls for patient endurance on the part of the saints who obey God's commandments and remain faithful to Jesus.

—Revelation 14:6–12

The Beast's Invasion of Israel

When the Beast breaks his covenant with Israel, what will prevent Israel from using nuclear warheads against this invasion by the Beast? If the Israelis truly have nuclear capabilities at this point, and with the knowledge that Israel will still be sovereign at that time, they would certainly use those weapons in a situation like this because they have vowed never again to let another Holocaust occur. Unfortunately, this question has no answer in Scripture—all we know for sure is that the Beast does "invade the Beautiful Land" (Dan. 11:41) and that the placement of the invasion has to be at the middle of the seven years, because he has to enter the Temple at that time and proclaim himself God (2 Thess. 2:3–4).

One possible scenario is that the Beast will claim the Egyptians are opposing him and inform Israel that he is planning to take out that nation. Because the Beast is Israel's protector at this time, they will give him permission to use their land as a staging area. After the Beast has defeated and looted Egypt, the Israelis will be caught off guard when the Beast's troops return to Israel and begin to take over military installations, power grids, communications, and government buildings.

This double-cross by the Beast will so surprise the Israeli leadership that the invasion will be nearly complete before they are able to organize any kind of meaningful resistance. The Beast's troops will penetrate Israel so quickly that the Israeli leadership won't be able to exercise their "Samson Option" by using nuclear bombs. Because most Israelis of military age carry a weapon and will no doubt be on alert during the Egyptian battle in order to safeguard against a counterattack, the invasion probably will not catch them completely off guard.

Daniel 11:41 states that when the Beast invades the Middle East at the mid-point of the seven years, Edom, Moab, and the leaders of Ammon will escape his conquest. Edom and Moab are now encompassed within the state of Jordan, and Ammon is the capital of Jordan. Somehow, God will protect Jordan for the sake of the Jewish remnant, who will flee to the deserts of Jordan to escape the persecution of the Beast (Rev. 12:14). Many believe this hideaway will be the ancient red-rock city of Petra.

God will protect this believing remnant of Israel for the last three and one-half years (Rev. 12:6). When the Beast realizes he can't destroy these individuals, he will turn and vent his rage on those in his empire who will not worship him (Rev. 12:17). Because the Beast is limited in his authority to those nations of Western Europe and some of the countries around the Mediterranean, he will not be able to touch the orthodox Jews, Christian believers, or Muslims in nations outside of his sphere of control.

The Two Witnesses

At the beginning of the last half of the seven years, two men will appear in Jerusalem and preach for 1,260 days (see Rev. 11:3). We know this event must occur during the last three and one-half years because God will give them the defensive weapon of fire from their mouths. (If they were to preach during the first half of the seven years, there would be no need for such a defensive weapon.) These two witnesses will preach in the streets of Jerusalem and will have the ability to send plagues and stop rain. As you may remember, God gave Moses the authority to send plagues upon the Egyptians, and He gave Elijah the authority to start and stop the rain in Israel (see 1 Kings 17:4; James 5:17–18).

At the end of the seven years, God will allow the Beast (indwelt by Satan) to kill the two witnesses. Their dead bodies will lie in the streets of Jerusalem for three and one-half days while people celebrate their deaths. At the end of this time, a voice will be heard from heaven saying, "Come up here." To the amazement and horror of those watching, the witnesses' decaying bodies will rise up from the ground and be taken up into the sky. At the same time, a severe earthquake will rock Jerusalem, destroying a tenth of the city and killing 7,000 people (see Rev. 11:7–13).

This earthquake takes place on the fourth day, after the end of the seven years. We know that it is the fourth day after the 1,260[th] day, because John says they will preach in the streets of Jerusalem for the last half of the seven years, or 1,260 days. They are killed on their last day of preaching, and lie in the street for three and one-half days. We are told in Revelation 11:13 that the people who see the two witnesses go into heaven and survive the earthquake are so awed that they give God praise. This is the only time we hear of anyone on earth praising God after the rapture of the church. This indicates the earthquake has to be of some magnitude in order to get people to come to the point of recognizing the hand of God.

No one knows the identity of the two witnesses. However, most Bible commentators agree that one of the witnesses will be Elijah the prophet, because in Malachi 4:5 the Lord states, "See, I will send Elijah before the great and dreadful day of the Lord comes." Some believe the other witness will be Enoch, because he was translated into heaven like Elijah. However, Enoch wasn't a Jew, which would present a problem because these men will only witness to the Jewish people, and it doesn't seem to make sense that God would send a non-Jewish witness to them.

The late J. Vernon McGee suggests this second witness may be John the Baptist:

> He was a forerunner of Christ at his first coming. He was similar to Elijah in manner and message. Both knew what it was to oppose the forces of darkness and stand alone for God against impossible odds. John the Baptist would be a witness of the New Testament, as Elijah would be for the Old Testament. John was not part of the church, the Bride of Christ, but he was a "friend of the bridegroom."[1]

Still others suggest the second witness will be Moses, as he would represent the Law and Elijah would represent the prophets, just as they did when they appeared with Jesus on the Mount of Transfiguration (Matt. 17:2–3). Again, there is no definite answer as to the identification of this second witness in Scripture.

The False Prophet

The False Prophet will become the high priest of emperor worship during the middle of the seven years. He will also be the enforcer of the Beast's edict of compulsory worship. His scheme to flush out believers will be to erect an image of the Beast on a wing of the Temple in Jerusalem and give it the ability to speak. All those in Israel who worship the image will live, while all those who don't will die (see Rev. 13:12–15). This is the "abomination that causes desolation" which Daniel warned about in Daniel 12:11 and of which Jesus spoke of in Matthew 24:15–16:

> So when you see standing in the holy place "the abomination that causes desolation," spoken of through the prophet Daniel—let the reader understand—then let those who are in Judea flee to the mountains.

To worship the Beast and take his mark will eliminate any possibility for a person ever to go heaven. (I know this was stated in an earlier chapter, but it is worth repeating here, as it is important to understand that the church will be on earth when this mark is required for survival.) Because of the severe persecution in Israel, most Jews who remain will make all kinds of compromises in order to placate the Beast.

The Final Solution

After the abomination is set up, the Beast and the False Prophet will then begin to track down anyone in the empire who will not worship the Beast by taking his mark. This will include Jews, Christians, and Muslims. No Muslim would dare take the mark, as it would mean he or she has submitted to worshiping the Beast. Because of this, it is quite possible that as the Beast destroys European churches in his empire, he will also destroy many European mosques. The Beast may be so confident in his satanic power at some point that he may even destroy the two mosques on the Temple Mount.

A professor of mine who had been a citizen of Nazi Germany told me that many Germans were glad to see the Jews sent away to the concentration camps because they felt, at the time, that the Jews owned just about everything in Germany. In the same way, many unbelieving Europeans will probably be relieved to see the elimination of Christians, Muslims, and Jews during the end times.

Anti-Semitism, promoted by the Roman Catholic Church, has always been present within the European psyche, and the elimination of born-again Christians could be seen as a welcome relief as Europeans shake off the shackles of the recently-destroyed, repressive church known in Revelation 17–18 as the harlot Babylon.

Likewise, the unbelieving Europeans may be pleased to see the extermination of Muslims. The Muslim population is exploding on the continent of Europe. Muslims comprise a significant voting bloc in Europe, and the leaders of Europe make it a point to cultivate their vote. By doing so, Europe is being taken over by Islam without a shot being fired. This does not go unnoticed by average Europeans, and their resentment towards Muslims continues to grow as this group demands more of their religious customs to be allowed and respected.

The killing of these millions of European Muslims will just add fuel to the Islamic world's hatred of the Beast. However, because the Beast will appear invincible at this time due to his supernatural powers, the Muslims will have to back off and wait for the right moment to retaliate. This will be the time when people will ask, "Who is like the Beast? Who can make war against him?" (Rev. 13:4).

The 144,000

Sometime before the wrath of God falls, a seal will be placed on the foreheads of 144,000 Jews, which will serve to protect them from the coming judgment. Twelve thousand men from each tribe of Israel, except the tribe of Dan (which will be replaced by the tribe of Joseph), will be protected in this way (see Rev. 7:4–8). Why will Dan be left out? One possible reason is because this tribe was the first to fall into idolatry during the time of the judges in Israel.

These 144,000 Jews are seen again in Revelation 14, when they stand in the heavenly Jerusalem/Mount Zion with Jesus. Revelation 14:3 states they have been "redeemed from the earth." This indicates they have all passed through death in order to be redeemed from the earth.

Many think the 144,000 are evangelists. This is probably true, but Scripture doesn't tell us what their purpose is. However, regardless of the reason for their being called out and marked by God, their work will be done within the borders of the Beast's domain. We know this is true, because if they were allowed to go throughout the world, not all of them would be killed by the Beast, as he does not have jurisdiction outside the areas of Western Europe and the Mediterranean Sea.

THE DAY OF THE LORD—THE WRATH OF GOD

Just before the Day of the Lord wrath the Beast's persecution will be "cut short" by the Beast himself. Most likely, he will be distracted by a report of the large and advancing armies of the King of the North and the kings of the East (Dan. 11:44). After taking time to mobilize and logistically manage his entire army, he will be left without the manpower to maintain his persecution.

Just after the Beast ends his persecution, he will be faced with the elements of the Wrath of God. These elements will consist of the sun's heat increasing to the point of scorching people, complete darkness in the Beast's domain, the seas turned to blood, and an outbreak of painful boils and plagues. This will slow his progress in meeting his enemies on the battlefield. God will also dry up the Euphrates River in order to give the troops from the East easy access to the state of Israel. Finally, at the end of the seven years, the Beast will charge out in a great rage to annihilate the invading troops. This battle will be engaged sometime during the thirty days after the seven years are completed (see Dan. 12:11).

I am convinced that the cosmic disturbances spoken of in Revelation will be of short duration and that they will occur before the rapture and the day-of-the-Lord wrath. I base this on the order of events given in Matthew 24:29–41, and the fact that the wrath of God takes the world by surprise. The rapture occurs sometime in the last half of the seven years, during the cosmic disturbances and just before the wrath of God falls. The rapture and the wrath take place on the same day. All the saints both living and dead will be caught up to be with the Lord. There is no partial rapture (see Matt. 24:29–31).

I want to emphasize again that the wrath of God is not the persecution of the Beast. The persecution is a time of oppression and terror by the Beast and the False Prophet and is aimed primarily at those who refuse to worship the Beast. The wrath of God is a separate period that begins shortly after the Beast's persecution has been "cut short," the cosmic disturbances have begun, and the rapture has taken place. Although the rapture takes place first, the rapture and the wrath of God occur the same day (see Rev. 6:10–11, 15–17).

The wrath of God is the day of the Lord. Walter K. Price, a Bible conference speaker, evangelist, and author of the book *The Prophet Joel and the Day of the Lord,* describes on whom the day of the Lord will fall:

> The nations on whom the day of the Lord will fall are those that have persecuted Israel. These Gentile persecutors have been represented by various nations in the past.... However, in the Book of Joel it was the Phoenicians and the Philistines, enemies of the covenant people in that day, whom the prophet typed as the great persecutors of Israel. Upon them was the day to come (Joel 3:4–8), for they had been especially hostile to the Jews. Upon them the day of the Lord will fall; however, they will only be the representatives of all those nations which have scattered and maltreated Israel. What is due the Phoenicians and the Philistines is also due the Edomites, Egyptians, Babylonians, Persians, Greeks, Romans, Russians, Nazis and the Arabs—all who have persecuted the covenant people of God.[2]

Dr. Price indicates that the wrath will only fall on those nations that have persecuted Israel. This could be true; however, the apostle Peter writes, "The day of the Lord will come like a thief. The heavens will disappear with a roar; the elements will be destroyed by fire, and the earth and everything in it will be laid bare" (2 Pet. 3:10). From this very clear statement, the day-of-the-Lord wrath appears to be a worldwide event. However, the wrath may be more heavily concentrated on those nations that have persecuted Israel.

The events of the wrath of God are in many ways an enigma to me. I believe they must be interpreted as John saw them and described them to us. I do not believe he was describing man-made planes, helicopters, and tanks, as some have said, because the wrath of God is entirely supernatural (see Rev. 9:1–11). A good example is seen in Revelation 9:13–16, where 200 million horses and riders are released in the River Euphrates by the four angels:

> The sixth angel sounded his trumpet, and I heard a voice coming from the horns of the golden altar that is before God. It said to the sixth angel who had the trumpet, "Release the four angels who are bound at the great river Euphrates." And the four angels who had been kept ready for this very hour and day and month and year were released to kill a third of mankind. The number of the mounted troops was two hundred million. I heard their number.

These are not human troops who come out of China to invade Israel, as some expositors believe. Even though these riders and their mounts have some resemblance to men and horses, we are told plainly in Revelation 9:20 that these are plagues, not human troops. It is also interesting to note that the colors of their breastplates match the colors of the plagues: yellow, the color of sulfur and brimstone; red, the color of fire; and blue, the color of smoke. Revelation 9:18 says, "A third of mankind was killed by the three plagues of fire, smoke and sulfur that came out of their mouths."

The one thing that must be remembered about the day-of-the-Lord wrath is that it consists entirely of God's wrath on unrepentant mankind. Humans do not instigate any part of the day-of-the-Lord wrath; they are just on the receiving end of it. God's wrath will be more devastating than any weapons humans could create, including nuclear weapons. A nuclear blast is instant death, whereas the wrath of God will be agonizing and painful. People will long to die but won't be able to do so (Rev. 16:10–11).

Pre-Armageddon

God takes no pleasure in the death of the sinner, and He is not willing that any should perish but that all should come to repentance (see 2 Pet. 3:9). The hearts of the people during this time must be very hard, for just after the last (seventh) trumpet judgment is given, Scripture states, "the rest of mankind that were not killed by these plagues still did not repent of the works of their hands" (Rev. 9:20).

The battle of Armageddon takes place after the seventh angel pours out the last bowl of judgment on mankind. When the Beast goes into the battle, he will no longer have supernatural powers, because his 1,260 days of empowerment will have run out (see Dan 11:7–12).

One of the reasons for placing the battle of Armageddon after the last bowl judgment is because it appears the Beast kills the two witnesses just before he loses his supernatural powers on the 1,260th day. The people of Jerusalem give gifts to one another and rejoice that the two are dead. These bystanders, who also see the resurrection of the two witnesses four days later, do not appear to be in any distress regarding an upcoming battle. This tells us the battle hasn't started yet. When the battle does start, the people of Jerusalem will be in great turmoil.

Summary

The first three and one-half years is a time of peace for both Europe and Israel. During this time, the Roman Catholic Church may bestow on the president of the European Union the title of "Emperor of the Holy Roman Empire." This will elevate President Delors and will enable the Roman Catholic Church to regain much of its lost glory and political power.

In the second half of the seven-year period, Satan will indwell President Delors, and he will become the man Scripture calls the "little horn." At this time he will destroy the Roman Catholic Church (because its leaders refuse to worship him) and install the imperial form of Roman government with its accompanying emperor worship. The False Prophet will enter the scene and act as high priest of worship for the emperor.

The Beast will then begin his wars of expansion by invading Egypt. Sudan and Libya will avoid destruction by submitting to the Beast. The Beast will turn north and invade Israel, ultimately entering the Temple in Jerusalem, where he proclaims himself to be God. This will begin the "time of Jacob's trouble." Believing Jews will flee to the desert of Jordan, where God will protect them for 1,260 days.

The persecution of the Jews, Muslims, and Christians will be cut short when the Beast learns the armies of the King of the North and the kings of the East are marching towards Israel. Immediately after the persecution, cosmic disturbances begin in the heavens. The rapture will take place the same day (but prior to) the Lord's wrath. After mobilizing his army, he will go out to fight a war from which he will never return. The war is the battle of Armageddon and will be fought during the thirty days after the seven-year period has run its course.

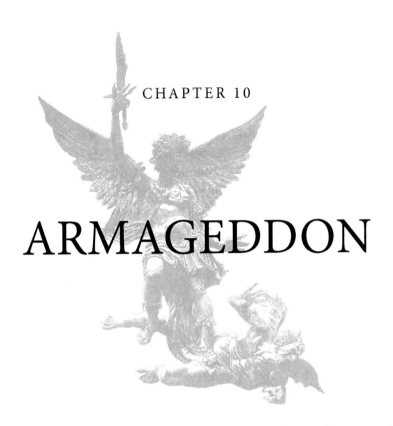

CHAPTER 10

ARMAGEDDON

The battle of Armageddon conjures up visions of apocalyptic, world-wide destruction. Motion pictures have used the word Armageddon to play on the angst of the general population to depict everything from alien invaders to falling meteorites. The Christian world has contributed to this distortion by supposing this war will be the "mother of all wars."

If one took Revelation 16:14 at face value, without considering the whole of Scripture, this would be an understandable mistake: "They are spirits of demons [frog like creatures] performing miraculous signs, and they go out to the kings of the whole world, to gather them for the battle on the great day of the Lord Almighty." If, however, the battle of Armageddon is viewed as part of God's judgment on those nations that have scattered and persecuted Israel throughout the centuries, and not the "whole world," it takes on an entirely different perspective.

As we've seen in previous chapters, the words "all earth" or "whole world" in Scripture often referred to a localized area that was known to the writer at that time. I believe John's description of the battle of Armageddon is a similar case in point. It will not include all the nations of the world but only those that have persecuted Israel.

This idea is not what has been taught down through the years. A simplified version of the commonly assumed scenario goes something like this: Sometime prior to the seven years, Russia and her Islamic allies will attempt an invasion of Israel. They are destroyed on the mountains of Israel by a mighty display of the power of God. At the end of the seven years, all the nations of the world will gather at a place in northern Israel called "Armageddon" to war against God and wipe out the little nation of Israel. The Lord returns, destroys the invaders, and sets up His millennial kingdom. Although this scenario is accepted as unsinkable, in my opinion, it's another Titanic, with only a few of the above events finding lifeboats.

Four Horns

In Zechariah 1:19–21, the prophet has a vision of four horns. When Zechariah asks the angel who is with him to explain the meaning of these four horns, the angel replies, "These are the horns that have scattered Judah, Israel and Jerusalem." Then the Lord shows Zechariah four craftsmen or carvers (the word "carvers" is an alternate translation for "craftsmen" and actually fits this situation better, as these four carvers come to destroy the four horns, not to build them up).

Zechariah asks the angel, "What are these coming to do?"

The angel answers, "These are the horns that scattered Judah so that no one could raise his head, but the craftsmen have come to terrify them and throw down the horns of the nations who have lifted up their horns against the land of Judah in order to scatter its people."

Reliable Bible authorities agree that the horns in this passage refer to the four Gentile powers in Nebuchadnezzar's dream in Daniel 2. The four traditional enemies of Israel have always been Babylon, Medo-Persia, Greece, and Rome. Today, the Gentile world that encompasses the same geographical areas as these four ancient empires did is still persecuting Jews: The Babylonian and Medo-Persian empires hold within their ancient boundaries much of the radical Islamic world today. Iraq encompasses much of the area of ancient Babylon, and modern-day Iran encompasses much of the territory of Medo-Persia. The Syrian fourth of Alexander the Great's Greek Empire was controlled by Antiochus Epiphanes, who forced the Greek culture and religion on the Jews. Today, Syria is considered a persecutor of Israel. The Roman Empire included most of the modern nations on the European continent and the countries around the Mediterranean. The Romans not only destroyed the Jewish Temple in 70 A.D. but also will, under the leadership of the Beast, desecrate the new (third) Temple and persecute the Jews in a manner never before seen in the history of the world.

Many people think that China will be part of the kings of the East who cross the dried-up Euphrates River in the invasion of Israel during the last days. However, China has not historically been a persecutor of Israel. And although there are some Muslims within the country, China is not considered to be a Muslim nation. The Chinese would have no real motivation to be involved in a war with Israel, except perhaps to profit as a supplier of weapons or to have territorial expansion after the war.

Russia (Magog) is the one exception to the geographical area theory of nations involved in the war. Russia is included because she has been a severe persecutor of Israel. As such, she comes under the judgment prophecies of those that have persecuted God's people. I believe this is why the Russian invasion of Israel, recorded in Ezekiel 38–39, is seen by most as being isolated from the battle of Armageddon, when in reality it is not.

A look at the Scriptural list of the combatant nations seems to confirm the theory that only the geographical area of the four ancient empires,(Babylon, Medo-Persia, Greece, and the revived Roman Empire) plus Russia and all the Islamic nations aligned with it, will be involved in the battle of Armageddon. This would *exclude* from the battle those countries that have not been persecutors of Israel, such as the United States, Great Britain, Mexico, Canada, the nations in Central and South America, Australia, New Zealand, China, and Japan.

The Combatants

As we mentioned at the beginning of this book, the EU has been reluctant to give Turkey membership into the Union. One of the main reasons for this (aside from the claim of Turkish human rights violations) is because Turkish membership would open the borders of Europe to a Muslim nation. This would cause huge problems, because

Muslim terrorists would freely be able to infiltrate Europe. Another reason the EU is wary of allowing Turkey to join the Union is because the nation would dominate the European political scene. Voting in the EU is based on a country's population, and because Turkey has a large population, it would have the largest voting bloc and be a significant threat to the other European members.

Because of the EU's refusal to admit Turkey as a member of the Union, it is highly probable that it will turn against the EU. In Ezekiel 38:5–6, the Lord, speaking against Magog, says, "Persia, Cush and Put will be with them, all with shields and helmets, also Gomer with all its troops, and Beth Togarmah from the far north with all its troops—the many nations with you." The location of Togarmah in this passage could be eastern Turkey (see Ezek. 27:14). While many believe that Gomer is Germany, it more likely refers to the Muslim areas of Croatia and Bosnia, as Germany is solidly locked into the European Union and thus already a combatant on the Beast's side at Armageddon. If we combine Croatia and Bosnia with the countries of Iraq, Iran, Syria, and the North African nations of Tunisia, Sudan, Ethiopia, Libya, and the "kings of the East" (India, Pakistan, Burma, and Sri Lanka), we have, for the most part, the nations' Scripture lists as the combatants against the Beast and the nation of Israel at the battle of Armageddon.

In opposition to these invaders of Israel are the Western European nations of the EU under the control of the Beast. The Beast, headquartered on the Temple Mount (see Dan. 11:45), will go out in a great rage to oppose the troops from the north and the other side of the Euphrates. In reality, he knows these forces are not only coming to eliminate Israel but also to seek revenge against him for the murder of millions of Muslims.

The Russian Invasion of Israel

As we've mentioned, most Bible authorities agree that Magog is Russia. The battle described in Ezekiel 38–39 is thus primarily an invasion of Israel by Russia and her allies. I believe this invasion is also the battle of Armageddon. However, this has caused a lot of problems for expositors, as they have attempted to place this event of Ezekiel 38–39 into the seven-year period.

One of the main problems scholars face is that Ezekiel states Israel will be at peace when Russia conceives the idea to invade it. According to most expositors, the entire seven years is to be a time of persecution, so Israel could not be at peace at any point during that time. In Ezekiel 38, the prophet, speaking against Gog, describes this time of peace:

> After many days you will be called to arms. In future years you will invade a land that has recovered from war, whose people were gathered from many nations to the mountains of Israel, which had long been desolate. They had been brought out from the nations, and now all of them live in safety.... You will say, "I will invade a land of unwalled villages; I will attack a peaceful and unsuspecting people—all of them living without walls and without gates and bars".... Therefore, son of man, prophesy and say to Gog: "This is what the sovereign LORD says: In that day, when my people Israel are living in safety, will you not take notice of it? You will come from your place in the far North, you and many nations with you, all of them riding on horses, a great horde, a mighty army."
>
> —Ezekiel 38:8, 11, 14–15

To resolve this problem of Israel being at peace, many expositors insist that the invasion in Ezekiel 38 is not the battle of Armageddon but a campaign that starts sometime before the seven years opens. The theory then assumes that God destroys Russia on the mountains of Israel before the seven years start (see Ezek. 39:1–6). The hordes coming from the North and the East in Daniel 11:44 would thus be troops coming from the east side of the Euphrates River that are headed for the battle of Armageddon at the end of the seven years. This theory is held by many well-known Bible scholars. J. Dwight Pentecost presents the following rationale for the theory:

> How could the beast have worldwide power if the power of the Northern Confederation has not been broken? The fact that the beast is in authority over the earth at the middle of the week lends support to the thesis that the king of the North has been destroyed. This destruction would produce a chaos in the world condition, which would bring the nations together as seen in Psalm 2, at which

time the government would be formed over which the beast is the head. Since there could be no unity of nations as long as the king of the North is operative, this unity must be brought about after his destruction.[1]

I would like to put forward a scenario concerning this invasion of Ezekiel 38–39. As mentioned above, Ezekiel 38:10–12 says that Israel will be at peace when Russia takes notice of it. This has to be sometime during the first three and one-half years, while Israel is sovereign and not being harassed by the Beast. Israel will be enjoying Temple worship and living in a pseudo peace with her neighboring Arab nations.

There may be a long period between the time Russia begins planning the invasion and the time it actually invades. In fact, Ezekiel 38:4 says that after the Russians get the idea for the invasion, they are so slow about putting the scheme into action that God puts hooks in their jaws to turn them around and head them in the right direction. We know these "hooks" are not literal. Some event or opportunity will draw them toward Israel at a particular time.

The Russian invasion of Israel will not be a rebellion against the Beast as some believe. Instead, Ezekiel 38:10–11 says that an "evil scheme" will come into the minds of those who live in the land of Magog. It is possible this evil scheme involves the Russians seeing an opportunity to seize Israel in order to acquire both a warm-water port and the valuable mineral deposits in the Dead Sea, or the rich oil deposits that are being found there. A major part of their strategy might be to use the Islamic *jihad* against Israel to accomplish this Machiavellian scheme. However, before they can complete their mobilization plans for the invasion, the Beast will begin the persecution and murder millions of European Muslims who refuse to take "the mark." The Islamic world will probably scream for revenge. This could be the "hooks in their jaws" that God uses to get Russia to move against Israel.

Unfortunately for the Russians, the European President will beat them to the punch by invading Israel first, and he will set up his headquarters in Jerusalem. This will create a twist in the Russian's original plans. They will realize that the Beast's new supernatural powers may equalize the playing field considerably and that extra care must be taken in mobilizing the largest and most effective force possible.

While the Russian and Islamic leaders ready their troops, the Beast's persecution of those who will not take his mark will turn Europe and Israel into a blood bath. The persecution will suddenly be "cut short"— perhaps because of the mobilization of the Russian and Islamic armies coming from the north and the Islamic armies coming from the east (see Dan. 11:44). The arrival of these armies will prove to be a major distraction for the Beast, and he will hurriedly have to cobble together an army, consisting of every able-bodied man in his empire. Even with his supernatural powers, he may not be able to stop this great horde of men and machines.

Soon after the persecution is "cut short," the rapture takes place and the wrath of God begins. The wrath makes it much more difficult for the armies on both sides to move logistically. This is the reason why I believe that they don't arrive on the battlefield until sometime during the thirty days after the seven years has run its course.

The Ezekiel Battle

Joel Rosenberg, author of the book *Epicenter*, believes that the war in Ezekiel 38–39 will take place before the seven years opens. He maintains this war could happen in the very near future and that it is not the battle of Armageddon. With all due respect to Mr. Rosenbberg, I believe that there are several one-time events depicted in Ezekiel 38–39 that can only occur after the battle of Armageddon has taken place.

One of these events is given in Ezekiel 38:23, where God says, "I will show my greatness and holiness, and I will make myself known in the sight of many nations." If the Lord were to make Himself known to Israel before the seven years, the Israelis would trust God rather than the Beast to be their protector during the first three and one-half years. They would look to God to do the same thing to those who want to destroy Israel as He did to the armies in the Ezekiel battle. According to the prophet Daniel, the Israelis will not rely on the Lord until after their dependence on man-made solutions is abolished. That occurs after the battle of Armageddon (see Dan. 12:7).

A second one-time event is the great feast of Ezekiel 39:4, where the carrion birds eat the flesh of the invading armies. This appears to be "the great supper of God" of Revelation 19. This feast only takes place once, and that is after the battle of Armageddon (see Ezek. 39:17–20; Rev. 19:17–18).

A third one-time event is depicted in Ezekiel 39:25, when the Lord brings Jacob (Israel) back to the land after this battle. The return of all Israel takes place only once, and that occurs only after the battle of Armageddon. It would be unthinkable that God would bring the Jews back to the land in order to be scattered by the Beast during the persecution.

A fourth one-time event is given in Ezekiel 39:26, where we read that the people of Israel will "forget their shame and unfaithfulness they have showed toward me." According to Daniel 9:24, this will only occur after the seventy "sevens" of years has passed, when Israel has completed its time of punishment.

I believe there is a fifth one-time event. It is the earthquake spoken of in Ezekiel 38:19–21. I am convinced that this is the same earthquake described in Revelation 16:17–20. The following is a presentation of the two Scripture passages for comparison:

In my zeal and fiery wrath I declare at that time there shall be a great earthquake in the land of Israel. The fish of the sea, the birds of the air, the beasts of the field, every creature that moves along the ground, and all the people on the face of the earth will tremble at my presence. The mountains will be overturned, the cliffs will crumble and every wall will fall to the ground.

—Ezekiel 38:19–20

The seventh angel poured out his bowl into the air, and out of the Temple came a loud voice from the throne, saying, "It is done!" Then there came flashes of lighting, rumblings, peals of thunder and a severe earthquake. No earthquake like it has ever occurred since man has been on earth, so tremendous was the quake. The great city split into three parts, and the cities of the nations collapsed…. Every island fled away and the mountains could not be found.

—Revelation 16:17–20

In the Ezekiel passage, the mountains are overturned. In the Revelation passage, the earthquake is said to be the greatest the world will ever experience. It is so great, in fact, that the mountains cannot be found. If there are two earthquakes, the first would send the Richter scale to heights no numbers have gone before, and eliminate any mountains being left for the second earthquake to destroy. It seems reasonable, therefore, to assume that both Ezekiel and Revelation are describing the same earthquake. This means the Russian invasion will take place at the time of the battle of Armageddon.

Egypt Is Missing

It is interesting to note that Egypt is not included with Sudan and Libya in the Ezekiel 38 battle. As I said, this battle is the battle of Armageddon, and as a Muslim nation, Egypt should be listed along-side the other Muslim nations. The reason the Egyptians are not listed among the allies of Gog is because the Beast crushes Egypt in the middle of the seven years (see Dan. 11:42–43). Sudan and Libya are not destroyed at that time because they submit to the Beast, and this submission gives them the opportunity to come later against the Beast when he is distracted by the northern and eastern hordes attacking him during the battle of Armageddon.

The fact that Egypt will be destroyed in the middle of the seven years is evidence that the Russian invasion of Israel will take place at the battle of Armageddon. If the Ezekiel battle were to take place before the seven years, Egypt would surely be included in the list of combatants in Ezekiel 38. The Beast's invasion of Egypt in the middle of the seven years is separated by a little more than three and one-half years from the Russian invasion of Israel during the battle of Armageddon.

The Location of the Battle

Those who believe the battle in Ezekiel occurs before the battle of Armageddon point to the fact that in the Ezekiel passage, the fighting takes place on the mountains of Israel and no mention is ever made to Armageddon. However, in Zechariah 14, which all agree describes the battle of Armageddon, the battle is seen taking place in Jerusalem. In the book of Revelation, the battle seems to take place at Armageddon in northern Israel. The point here is that even though these armies seem to be located in different places, they are still part of the battle of Armageddon, and all of the armies will be judged at the battle of Armageddon.

With the evidence just presented, I believe it must be concluded that the battle depicted in Ezekiel 38–39 is the battle of Armageddon.

The Real War

Revelation 19:19 says, "Then I saw the Beast and the kings of the earth and their armies gathered together to make war against the rider on the horse [the Lord Jesus] and his army." How would it be possible for these human armies, who are gathered at Armageddon, to believe they could wage war against the God of the universe? Surely, the leaders of these armies wouldn't think they would be able to defeat an all-powerful, all-knowing God with their man-made weapons. It doesn't take a lot of intelligence to know that physical beings are no match for spiritual beings and that a war cannot be waged against them with conventional weapons. Realizing this, we have to determine that Satan's attempt to gather the kings of the earth together at Armageddon to war against God must have some meaning other than a literal one.

As we mentioned, Satan has been fighting down through the ages against the archangel, Michael, and at the middle of the seven years is finally thrown from heaven down to earth (see Rev. 12:7–12). He then incarnates himself in the Beast, demands worship from all those under his control, and attempts to rid his territory of all those who won't worship him as God. This is Satan's war against God.

The armies of the North and of the East who fight against the Beast by invading Israel are, in reality, also fighting against God. Israel is "the apple of God's eye" (Zech. 2;8), and He always judges those who come against her. The invaders think they are there to kill Jews and defeat the Beast. None of the combatants, the Beast's troops included, have any idea that they are fighting against the God of heaven.

At Christ's return (Revelation 19:11–16), He is seen with His angels in a figurative representation of Him defeating the armies at the battle of Armageddon. Revelation 19:15 tells us that the Lord destroys all these armies by a sword that comes from His mouth. Of course, this is not a literal sword. The Word of the Lord has always been "sharper than any double-edged sword" (Heb. 4:12). In an instant, all the prophecies of the Word of God for the destruction of these end-times invaders of Israel, along with the Beast's troops will become a reality. What was prophesied against these invading armies in Zechariah, Joel, Ezekiel, and Revelation will become destruction for the Arabs, Russians, eastern armies of the old colonial Indian Empire, and the armies of the Beast.

As these armies are fighting among themselves, a strange disease will come over them and their animals, which will cause them to rot in their very tracks (Zech. 14:12). This could be similar to what happened to the Nazi agent in *Raiders of the Lost Ark* when he looked into the Ark of the Covenant and his flesh melted on the spot.) The Lord will also send huge hailstones, torrents of rain, and burning sulfur. The destruction will be so extensive that it is difficult for humankind to comprehend.

The Battle in Perspective

While the following passage in Daniel 11:36–43 does not describe the battle of Armageddon, I have included it here to make a comment concerning the prevailing interpretation of the actions of the Beast:

> The king will do as he pleases. He will exalt and magnify himself above every god and will say unheard-of things against the God of gods. He will be successful until the time of wrath is completed, for what has been determined must take place. He will show no regard for the gods of his fathers or for the one desired by women, nor will he regard any god, but will exalt himself above them all. Instead of them, he will honor a god of fortresses; a god unknown to his fathers he will honor with gold and silver, with precious stones and costly gifts. He will attack the mightiest fortresses with the help of a foreign god and will greatly honor those who acknowledge him. He will make them rulers over many people and will distribute the land for a price.
>
> At the time of the end the king of the South will engage him in battle, and the king of the North will storm out against him with chariots and cavalry and a great fleet of ships. He will invade many

countries and sweep through them like a flood. He will also invade the Beautiful Land. Many countries will fall, but Edom, Moab and the leaders of Ammon will be delivered from his hand. He will extend his power over many countries; Egypt will not escape. He will gain control of the treasures of gold and silver and all the riches of Egypt, with the Libyans and Nubians in submission.

In this passage, the angel is describing to Daniel what will happen at the end of the corridor of this age. Daniel views these events on a flat surface and not chronologically, which means that he doesn't necessarily see the events in relation to time. For example, in verse 40, where Daniel notes the time of the end, he sees the king of the South [Egypt] and the king of the North coming out to engage the Beast in battle. What Daniel doesn't see is the indeterminate period of time that separates the Beast's conquest of Egypt from the fight with the king of the North at the battle of Armageddon.

To put the events in chronological order, we must gather information from other parts of the Bible. When the Beast becomes Satan incarnate and demands worship as God in the middle of the seven years, he will ruthlessly crush Egypt (the king of the South) and take all the Egyptian treasures (see Dan. 11:42–43). As already stated, Sudan and Libya will simply submit to the overwhelming power of the supernatural Beast and his superior army (see Dan. 11:43.) After the Beast invades Egypt, he will turn north and overrun Israel (see Dan. 11:41).

During this invasion of Israel, the Beast will force his way into the Temple and sit on the mercy seat between the golden cherubim, where he will proclaim himself to be Emperor God (see 2 Thess. 2:3–4; Rev. 11:2). Daniel 11:45 says the Beast will make his headquarters on the Temple Mount. The Beast is stopped by the Lord from invading Jordan (Edom, Moab, and the leaders of Ammon). This, I believe, is for the sake of the believing remnant of Jews, who are being protected there (see Rev. 12:6, 14–16; Dan. 1 1:41).

Later, the Beast will hear an alarming report that the armies of the kings of the East and the king of the North are coming toward Jerusalem (see Rev. 16:12; Ezek. 38:15; Dan. 11:40). Daniel 11:44 says that this report from the east and the north alarms him. I don't blame him: By this time, the four-headed leopard nations of Pakistan, Burma, Sri Lanka, and

India (see Dan. 7:6) will have a population of over 1.25 billion. Add in millions more for the Russian and Islamic forces of the Middle East, and the size of the combined armies will become a serious problem for him.

The Beast will go out in a great rage to destroy the invading armies. Daniel 11:45 makes the comment that the Beast will come to his end and that no one will stand with him. This implies that there are nations other than those coming against him that are not under his control.

The Expositor's Dilemma

A problem arises for expositors if the invasion of Israel in Daniel 11:41 is not interpreted as an invasion by the Beast during the middle of the seven years. The reason expositors fail to place this invasion during the middle of the seven years is because they believe the Beast will be accepted as the Messiah by the Jews. They believe that the Beast, presenting himself as the Messiah, will enter the Temple in the middle of the seven years with Israel's blessing. Thus, there would be no need for an invasion by the Beast at any time. They therefore conclude that the invasion of Israel in Daniel 11:41 must be at a different time and by someone other than the Beast. This particular mindset forces a "pieced-together" scenario to fit the events of Daniel 11.

A possible way out of this dilemma can be found in Daniel 11:41, where the pronoun "he" appears to be connected to the king of the North. The assumption made regarding the "he" of Daniel 11:41 is that the pronoun refers to the Beast from verses 36 through 40 and then changes in Verse 41 to represent the king of the North. This interpretation is based on the English rule of grammar that states the pronoun refers back to the nearest antecedent, which in this case would be the king of the North. However, it is interesting to note that the original writings and translations of the Scriptures were done before the invention of English rules of grammar, and this rule does not always apply in Scripture. An example of one Scripture passage that does not follow this English grammatical rule can be found in Acts 18:18:

> Paul stayed on in Corinth for some time. Then he left the brothers and sailed for Syria, accompanied by Priscilla and Aquilla. Before he sailed, he had his hair cut off at Cenchrea because of a vow he had taken.

To follow this rule, Aquilla would be the one who, before he sailed, cut off his hair because of a vow. However, we know that Paul is the primary character of the text, and it is Paul to whom the sentence refers. The same sentence structure applies to the "he" in Daniel 11:41.

I maintain that the pronoun representing the Beast is followed from Daniel 11:36 to the end of the chapter. The subject to whom the "he" refers in the second half of Daniel 11:41 is ambiguous—it could refer to the Beast (the subject of the preceding paragraph) or to the king of the North (the subject of the preceding sentence). I don't think the subject is the King of the North, because the chapter is talking about the Beast, not the King of the North. It would be strange indeed for the whole chapter to refer to the Beast and just in that one verse the "he" refer to the king of the North.

The Destruction of Jerusalem

The Scriptures seem to indicate that the invading armies will gather at Armageddon but the main thrust of the fighting will be in Jerusalem. In Zechariah 14:2, the Lord tells the prophet, "I will gather all the nations to Jerusalem to fight against it; the city will be captured, and the houses ransacked, and the women raped. Half the city will go into exile, but the rest of the people will not be taken from the city." Jerusalem will be split into three parts by an earthquake during this time, and many Jews will escape the slaughter taking place in Jerusalem by the invading armies (Zech. 14:2), by fleeing down through the deep ravine into the valley made by this earthquake (Zech. 14:4–5). The new valley may be the valley of Jehoshaphat (see Joel 3:2), where God will judge the nations ("Jehoshaphat" means "God judges"). The present so-called Valley of Jehoshaphat is a ravine and not a valley, so it is improbable that this is the valley of Jehoshaphat spoken of in Joel. The valley of Jehoshaphat will no doubt be a future valley in Israel.

Jerusalem will be devastated by these invading hordes. But then, just at the crucial moment, when it appears all is lost and Jerusalem completely destroyed, Jesus will return to earth, and He will stand on the Mount of Olives, the very place He ascended to heaven approximately 2,000 years earlier (see Acts 1:10–11).

According to Revelation 19:11–16 Jesus will be wearing many crowns, and riding a white horse, is followed by the armies of God, and is victor over the nations at the battle of Armageddon. I believe this is a symbolic representation of Jesus as victor. His actual physical return will be at the Mount of Olives (Acts 1:10–12).

As Jesus touches down, the Mount of Olives will be split in two from east to west (see Zech. 14:4). At this time, Jesus will destroy all the armies fighting in Israel from the plains of Armageddon to all points south of Jerusalem. Instantly, all the prophecies against the enemies of Israel will be fulfilled.

Revelation 14:20 says that the blood from this war will be as high as a horse's bridle from Dan to Beersheba, a distance of approximately 150 miles. Ezekiel 38 says there will be many horses ridden by the northern forces, and the bodies of these dead animals will no doubt contribute to the volume of blood in this "dead sea." This statement about the blood could just be hyperbole, meaning this will be an extremely bloody war.

In Revelation 19:20, we see that at the battle the Beast will be captured along with the False Prophet and that both of them will be thrown *alive* into the fiery lake of burning sulfur. Daniel gives us a slightly different slant on the disposal of the Beast. He says the Beast will be *slain* and that his *body* will be destroyed and then he is thrown into the blazing fire. This occurs during a judgment that takes place after the four beasts of Daniel 7 have had their authority to rule taken from them by the Lord Jesus. We see that the Beast's body is destroyed but that his soul is thrown into the lake of fire. Satan is separated from the body of the Beast and is thrown into the Abyss for 1,000 years (Rev. 20:1–3).

The Victor

Daniel 11:45 states that the Beast "will come to his end, and no one will help him." This implies that there will be nations other than those in battle against the Beast that are not aligned with him and could come to his assistance, but that they will not do so. These nations could be the lioness, Great Britain, and her "cubs." They will probably distance themselves from the EU and its leader when they realize that he has become a ruthless dictator. There is also the fact that because of the plagues from the wrath of God that have fallen on the earth at this time, the nations will be hard-pressed to care for themselves, much less to come to the aid of another nation or ruler.

After the battle, the Lord is seen coming out of Edom covered with blood (see Isa. 63:1–6). This may be a picture of the victorious Jesus leading the remnant of Jewish believers home from their desert hiding place, as the prophet Zechariah says that after the war there will be a great ingathering of the Jews:

> Though I scatter them among the peoples, yet in the distant lands they will remember me. They will return. I will bring them back from Egypt and gather them from Assyria. I will bring them back to Gilead and Lebanon, and there will not be room enough for them.
> —Zechariah 10:9–10

Seventy-five Days

In Daniel 12:11–12, the angel tells Daniel, "From the time that the daily sacrifice is abolished and the abomination that causes desolation is set up, there will be 1,290 days. Blessed is the one who waits for and reaches the end of the 1,335 days."

The day that Jesus physically touches down on the earth will begin the Jewish Day of Atonement (Yom Kippur). We know that this will be Yom Kippur because at Christ's return, atonement is made for sin (Dan.9:24). The Jews will realize that Jesus is both the sacrificial lamb and the scapegoat who takes away their sin. The whole nation of Israel will repent for their rejection of Jesus, their Messiah. This mourning may be much like the mourning Joseph's brothers did when they found out the ruler of Egypt was really their brother whom they thought they had killed. As Zechariah 12:9–10 states:

> I will pour out on the house of David and the inhabitants of Jerusalem a spirit of grace and supplication. They will look on me, the one they have pierced, and they will mourn for him as one mourns an only child, and grieve bitterly for him as one grieves for a first-born son.

This mourning by the Jews will be different from the mourning the nations of the world will do when they see the Son of Man returning just after the persecution has been cut short. At that time, the nations will mourn the fact that they are in serious trouble because of the wrath of God (see Rev. 6:15–17).

Jesus, who will be priest and king after the order of Melchizedek (Hebrews 6:20), will discard all the desecrated rubble of the persecution Temple that the great earthquake left behind and will build the millennium Temple after the pattern given in Ezekiel. God's words in Zechariah 6:12–13 confirm this:

> Tell him this is what the LORD Almighty says: "Here is the man whose name is the Branch, and he will branch out from his place and build the Temple of the LORD. It is he who will build the Temple of the Lord, and he will be clothed with majesty and will sit and rule on his throne. And he will be a priest on his throne. And there will be harmony between the two."

This new Temple will be dedicated at the end of a seventy-five-day period, which will be from the Day of Atonement (Yom Kippur) to the Celebration of Lights (Hanukkah). Hanukkah is the celebration of the cleansing and rededication of the Temple after it was desecrated by Antiochus Epiphanes. These seventy-five days, when added to 1,260 days, total 1,335 days. Of these seventy-five days, the first thirty contain the battle of Armageddon and Yom Kippur. At the end of the 1,290 days, the transgression will be finished. There will be an end of sin, atonement for wickedness will be made, everlasting righteousness will come in, visions and prophecy will be sealed up, and the most holy will be anointed (see Dan. 9:24).

The following forty-five days are designated by Scripture for the restoration of the land and preparation of the surviving Jews for their separation unto the Lord (see Dan 12:11–12). This is why the Scriptures say "blessed is the one who waits for and reaches the end of the 1,335 days" (Dan. 12:12). Only those who have repented of their sins and have believed Jesus is the Son of God will be allowed to go into the millennial kingdom (Matt. 25:).

Ezekiel 39:12 states that it will take seven months to bury all the bodies and cleanse the land. People will be employed to find bones and set up markers so that the grave diggers (who will be ceremonially unclean) can come along and collect and bury them.

Jesus' millennial reign on earth will be the beginning of a new age of peace on earth for 1,000 years (Rev. 20:1–3).

Summary

The focus of the battle of Armageddon will be the nation of Israel. This battle will not only be a judgment on the nations that have persecuted Israel but also a judgment on Israel itself. The four traditional enemies of Israel have always been Babylon, Medo-Persia, Greece (which includes the old Indian Empire nations), and the ancient Roman Empire. The modern nations that will be involved in this war will be within the geographical areas of these four ancient empires. The only country not within this geographical area that will be included in the conflict is Russia. Russia is included because it qualifies as a great persecutor of Israel. As such, it comes under prophetical judgment regarding those that have persecuted God's people.

Because the EU has been reluctant to give Turkey membership into the Union, the Turkish government may turn against the Beast and the EU. If we combine the country of Turkey with that of Croatia, Bosnia, Iraq, Iran, Syria, Tunisia, Sudan, Ethiopia, Libya, India, Pakistan, Burma, and Sri Lanka, we have the nations the Bible lists as combatants against the Beast and Israel at the battle of Armageddon. These nations will join with Russia in the battle. Notably missing from this alliance is Egypt, a Muslim nation, which will be destroyed by the Beast in the middle of the seven years.

A long period may elapse between the time the Russians begin planning the invasion and the time they actually carry it out. Before they can complete their plans for mobilization, the Beast will begin the persecutions. The murder of millions of European Muslims could be the "hooks in their jaws" that God uses to get Russia and her Muslim allies to move against Israel.

The invasion will divert the Beast's attention and "cut short" the persecutions. Even with his supernatural powers, he may not be able to stop the great horde of men and machines with which he is confronted. Shortly after, the rapture will take place and the Wrath of God will begin (Matthew 24:36–41).

When Jesus touches down at the Mount of Olives, it will split in two from east to west, and all the prophecies of the Lord for the destruction of these end-times invaders of Israel will become a reality (Zech. 14:4). A strange disease will come over the armies as they are fighting among themselves, which will cause them to rot in their tracks. They will also be confronted with hailstones, torrents of rain, and burning sulfur. All the armies fighting in Israel from the plains of Armageddon to all points south of Jerusalem will be destroyed by the Word of the Lord.

The Beast and the False Prophet will be captured and thrown into the Lake of Fire. Satan will be separated from the Beast and thrown into the Abyss for 1,000 years. Jerusalem will be split into three parts, and many Jews will escape the holocaust caused by the invading armies by fleeing down through the deep ravine into the valley made by the earthquake. The Jews will realize that Jesus is the Messiah, and the whole nation will repent.

Jesus will discard the desecrated rubble of the persecution Temple and establish the millennium Temple. His millennial reign on earth will be the beginning of a new age of peace on earth for 1,000 years.

CONCLUSION

Beyond a shadow of a doubt, we have crossed over the threshold of the Apocalypse. The first president of the EU will soon receive the kingdom of the ten horns (the ten nations of the EU) as prophesied in Revelation 17:13. We know that the Apocalypse is upon us because these events will never happen again in Western Europe, as there will be no longer ten independent nations in Western Europe to unify a second time to fulfill this prophecy.

The next prophetic event moving the world toward the return of Christ will be the covenant that the president of the EU will make with Israel.

What an opportunity Christians have for reaching out to an unbelieving world! It is now possible to open the Word of God and point to the fact that there is a God in heaven who is involved in the present-day affairs of men, and that what He has written is becoming a reality in our time.

Pastor Mark Blitz, founder of El Shaddai Ministries, went on NASA's website to see if he could discover any solar eclipses or lunar eclipses that might be significant for biblical prophecy. He was surprised to discover a rare and uncanny cluster of four lunar eclipses and two solar eclipses around the Jewish sabbatical year of 2014/2015. Further, he found that the majority of them landed on important Jewish holy days: The Feast of Trumpets/Rosh Hashanah (September/October), the Day of Atonement/Yom Kippur (September/October), and the Feast of Tabernacles/Ingathering (September/October).

Alan Kurschner, commenting on Biltz's findings in an article for Prewrath Rapture Dot Com, states, "The four spring feasts of the Lord were fulfilled prophetically during the first coming of Christ. And Prewrath teaches that the three remaining fall feasts will be fulfilled during Christ's second coming.... And the Bible clearly teaches that a particular cluster of cosmic disturbances including the sun and moon will be a sign of the second coming." From what we now know about the end times, these eclipses could not be related to the cosmic disturbances of Matthew 24:29 and the sixth seal of Revelation 6:12.[1]

When I was a new believer, I used to think that the most exciting time to be alive would have been during the Exodus. How thrilling it would have been to have seen the miracles God performed when He was bringing the children of Israel out of Egypt. However, as the years have passed, and now knowing what God is going to do in the near future, the Exodus seems to pale by comparison.

Scriptures say we can't know the day or the hour of the rapture, but I believe we can know *approximately* when it will occur. This is possible because the Word gives us various clues about the events that will occur before the rapture takes place. By now, I'm sure you realize that we are much closer to the end than many people think. So, are you ready to be part of the celebration in heaven, or will you be one who will experience the wrath of God?

The purpose of this book has been to awaken each of us to the fact that the Apocalypse has begun. The Living God will be coming soon to judge sinful mankind. These are sobering days, and it is my desire and prayer that those who read this book will be challenged to structure their lives to be "good and faithful servants." The time is short. The stakes are high—they are the very stakes of life and death.

ENDNOTES

Chapter 1: The Fourth Beast of the Apocalypse

1. All citizens of the European Union member states have the right to vote and are eligible for political office. They can also vote in the EU state in which they live, even if they are citizens of another member state. The wheels of this lumbering and sometimes stumbling organization are moved along by four governing bodies: (1) the Council of Ministers, (2) the Commission, (3) the Parliament, and (4) the Court of Justice.

   The heads of state of the member countries formed the first governing body, **the Council of Ministers**. Every six months the presidency of the European Union would rotate among the heads of state. At the end of each six-month period, the Council of Ministers would hold a summit meeting in the country of the presiding president. Under the Lisbon Treaty (constitution), the Council will have a permanent president who will be appointed by the Council for a two and one-half year, renewable term.

   The Commission: The second body, the European Commission, is located in Brussels, Belgium, and is the executive branch of the EU. The Commission in reality is not a governing body; its place is more of a steering position. The Commission forms legislation and coordinates the different interests of the member countries, such as agriculture, transportation, immigration, exportation, trade, and so forth. Some twenty to thirty commissioners surround the president of the Commission. They carry the portfolios of the different interests mentioned above and appointed by their particular country's head of state. The president of the Commission assigns the portfolios each carries. Under the new constitution, the Parliament will appoint the president of the Commission. Some 20,000 "Eurocrats" are the worker bees who take the directives from the president of the Commission and flesh them out into legislation to be given to the third governing body, the European Parliament, based in Strasbourg, France.

The European Parliament. The members of Parliament are elected by their respective countries for a term of four years. Before the Intergovernmental Conference (IGC) of 1996, the Parliament was little more than a debating club. New power for the Parliament was more or less forced upon the Council because the rank and file of Europe felt the EU hierarchy was not open enough in the decisions that were being made by the small group of national leaders. After leaving the Parliament, all legislation goes to the Council of Ministers for consideration. Legislation now goes to the President for his approval.

The Court of Justice. The European Court of Justice is composed of thirteen judges and is housed in Luxembourg. The court mainly decides issues concerning trade and business conflicts involving both governments and individuals—such things as fishing rights, who pays for the use of what roads, and so forth. Decisions made by the Commission and the Council of Ministers are directly applicable to the member states and must be applied to both national administrations and national courts. These decisions may be challenged before the Court of Justice, which ensures that EU law is interpreted in the same way throughout the Community. EU law negates national law when they are in contradiction.

2. James M. Markham, "Europe Looks to '92 as Dreams of Union Come True," *TheNew York Times*, July 15, 1988.

3. Steven Greenhouse, "U.S. Companies See 1992 as Opportunity," *San Jose Mercury News*, March 26, 1989.

4. Denise Claveloux, "Use the ECU," *Europe*, November 1989. Excerpted by permission of *Europe*. Subscriptions $19.95 each year from *Europe*, 2100 M Street, NW, 7th floor, Washington, D.C., 20037.

5. Charles C. Ryrie, *The Ryrie Study Bible* (Chicago, IL: Moody Bible Institute of Chicago, 1979), 1895. Used by permission.

Chapter 2: The Beast of the Apocalypse

1. John Ardagh, "Will the New Europe Please Sit Down," *TheNew York Times*, November 10, 1991.

2. Charles Grant, *Delors, Inside the House That Jacques Built* (London: Nicholas Brealey Publishing Ltd., 1994), 115.

3. Ibid., 25.

4. Ardaugh, "Will the New Europe Please Sit Down."

5. Charles Grant, *Delors, Inside the House That Jacques Built*, 246.

6. Ibid., 168.

7. Ibid., 236.

8. Ibid., 38.

9. Ibid., 43.

10. Ibid., 162.

11. Ibid., 240

12. Ibid., 256

13. Ibid.

Chapter 3: The Dual Origins of the Beast

1. Tim La Haye, *Revelation Unveiled* (Grand Rapids, MI: Zondervan Publishing, 1999). 215

Chapter 4: Persecution During the Apocalypse

1. Henry Clarence Thiessen, *Introductory Lectures in Systematic Theology* (Grand Rapids, MI: William B. Eerdmans, 1949), 480.

2. Hal Lindsey, *There's a New World Coming* (Eugene, OR: Harvest House, 1984), 104. Used by permission.
3. Marvin J. Rosenthal, *The Pre-Wrath Rapture of the Church* (Nashville, TN: Thomas Nelson, 1990), 103–105.
4. John McLean, "The Chronological and Sequential Structure of the Book of Revelation" (a position paper presented to the Pretrib Research Center in Washington, DC), 21.
5. J. Dwight Pentecost, *Things to Come* (Findlay, OH: Durham Publishing Company, 1958), 279. Used by permission of Zondervan Publishing House.

Chapter 5: The Rapture of the Church

1. Marvin J. Rosenthal, *The Pre-wrath Rapture of the Church* (Nashville, TN: Thomas Nelson, 1990), 205–206.
2. Text by: Charles Wesley, Music by: Thomas Campbell, choral ending: Joseph Linn. c.1986 "And Can It Be" (hymn) Norman Clayton Pub. A division of Word, 1986

Chapter 6: The Four Great Beasts of the Apocalypse

1. *The Amplified Bible*, adapted note from the Homiletic Commentary (Grand Rapids, MI: Zondervan Publishers, 1965), 1052.
2. Henry M. Morris, *The Revelation Record* (Wheaton IL: Tyndale House Inc., 1983), 235.
3. C. I. Scofield wrote that Daniel's vision in chapter 7 was the same vision that Nebuchadnezzar had in chapter 2 but with a slightly different twist. Where Nebuchadnezzar saw the magnificence of the "times of the Gentiles," Daniel saw the raw and warlike nature of the Gentile nations.
4. Jamison, Fausset, and Brown, *Commentary on the Whole Bible* (Grand Rapids, MI: Zondervan Publishers, 1961), 748.

Chapter 7: The Identity of the Four Beasts

1. Derek Prince, "Our Debt to Israel" (Charlotte, NC: Derek Prince Ministries, A short track. 1998).
2. Gale Research, *Countries of the World* (Tower Books. Detroit MI).

3. Charles Thomson, translator, and C.A. Muse, editor, *The Septuagint Bible* (Indian Hills, CO: Falcon's Wing Press, 1954), 1338.

4. George Otis Jr., *The Last of the Giants* (Tarrytown, NY: Chosen Books, 1991), 202. Used by permission.

5. Andrew Sullivan, "Britain Is a Natural Born NAFTA Nation," *The European*, December 16–24, 1997, 12.

6. *Las Vegas Sun,* January 17, 2009, 5

7. *San Francisco Chronicle,* November 11, 1989.

8. *The World Almanac* (Pleasantville, NY: World Almanac Books, 2009), 715–717.

9. Brahma Chellancy, "Passage to Power," *Monitor*, February 1990, 24. Used by permission of the author.

Chapter 8: Mystery Babylon

1. J. Vernon McGee, Notes on Revelation (Through the Bible Radio Publisher).

2. Walter K. Price, *The Prophet Joel and the Day of the Lord* (Chicago, IL: Moody Press, 1976), 90–91. Used by permission.

Chapter 9: Conclusion

1. J. Dwight Pentecost, *Things to Come* (Findlay, OH: Durham Publishing Company, 1958), 353–354. Used by permission of Zondervan Publishing House.

GLOSSARY OF TERMS

144,000, the: Twelve thousand Jews from each tribe of Israel, excluding the tribe of Dan. Joseph replaced the tribe of Dan.

Abyss: A place of confinement prepared for Satan and his minions.

Abomination of Desolation: The setting up of an image or statue in the Temple at Jerusalem that will be demonically empowered to speak.

Advent: Derived from the Latin word "*adventus*," which means "arrival, coming, or presence." It is used to speak both of Jesus' first coming and His second coming.

Ammon: The capital of the state of Jordan.

Antichrist: An expression used in 1 and 2 John to describe the man or spirit against Christ; also, the popular name for the Beast of Revelation and Daniel.

Antiochus Epiphanes: ruled the Syrian fourth of Alexander the Great's Empire; a type of the Beast, who will rule the revived Roman Empire.

Aorist tense: The default tense in the Greek language.

Apocalypse: Derived from the Greek *apokalypsis,* meaning "unveiling or revealing." It is a popular definition for some kind of world catastrophic event, but it can also refer to a prophetic disclosure or the last book of the New Testament (The Apocalypse of John or The Revelation of Jesus Christ).

Armageddon: The war described in Revelation 19, Daniel 11, and Ezekiel 38–39; the last great battle at the end of this age, said to be fought in a valley in Northern Israel.

Artaxerxes: The Persian king who issued the decree to rebuild Jerusalem and allowed the Jews to return to the land during the time of Daniel.

Belshazzar: The last king of the Neo-Babylonian Empire.

Constitution (of the EU): known as the Lisbon Treaty.

Delors, Jacques: President of the EU Commission from 1984 to 94. The first president of a unified Europe whom Scripture identifies as the Beast.

Dragon, the: A representation of Satan.

Etruscans: A people of Asia Minor who migrated to Italy, bringing with them the mother/son religion.

Beast, the: The individual popularly known as the Antichrist. Other names include: the little horn, the man of Lawlessness, and the man of sin. The man known as the Beast is represented in Scripture as a combination of two governments—the ten-horned government and the imperial form of government.

Beasts: Used in Scripture to denote an entity that has rejected God's rule. A biblical beast may be a man or a kingdom and represent a combination of two or more governments.

Bear, the: One of the four beasts depicted in Daniel 7; believed to be communist Russia.

Crowns: Symbolic of power and authority or sovereignty.

Day of the Lord: A special time of wrath against an unbelieving and unrepentant world. This begins shortly after the persecution has been cut short sometime during the last seven years; also known as the day-of-the-Lord wrath.

Diaspora: The dispersion of the twelve tribes of Israel into all the world. The diaspora represents the time during which Israel is out of the land and ends when God brings them back after the battle of Armageddon.

European Union (EU): An organization of European nations that began in 1957 with six nations signing the Treaty of Rome, and emerged as the ten-horned confederacy of Revelation 17:12–13 with the birth of the European Single Market in 1992. Past names include the European Economic Community and the European Community.

European Currency Unit (ECU): The monetary system of the EU, now known as the "Euro."

Emperor, the: Designation for the Beast when the Pope of Rome crowns him Emperor of the Holy Roman Empire.

Eurocrats: Some 20,000 non-elected officials who work at the EU headquarters in Brussels, Belgium.

Eschatology: The study of last things.

False Prophet: The one who "comes from the earth" during the last days to enforce the worship of the Beast. This being does not arrive on the world scene until the middle of the seven years. He will take on the garb of a religious leader (not the Pope, because the Roman Church will be destroyed about this time) and have great power and authority.

Gentile Nations: All nations of the world that are not a part of the twelve tribes of Israel.

Gomer: Son of Japheth, son of Noah. Gomer is believed to have located in the area of Germany, or possibly Croatia and Bosnia..

Hades: Abode of the unbelieving dead waiting for the day of judgment.

Horn: Symbolic of a king or kingdom or power and authority.

Jacob's trouble: A time of persecution and disruption; known as the tribulation (persecution).

Jihad: Islam's continuing war against the non-Muslim world.

King of the North: Thought to be the leader of Russia.

King of the South: The ruler of Egypt.

Kings of the East: Those nations that composed the Old Colonial Indian Empire—Pakistan, Burma, India, and Sri Lanka.

Lisbon Treaty: The final treaty that unified the EU.

Lake of Fire: The final place of confinement for the Beast, False Prophet, Satan, demons, and all unbelievers.

Lamb, the: The Lord Jesus Christ, who was slain from the creation of the world for the sins of mankind (Rev. 13:8).

Leopard, the: One of the four beasts depicted in Daniel 7; believed to be a symbolic representation of the old colonial Indian Empire, which consisted of India, Sri Lanka, Pakistan, and Burma. This empire was ruled by Britain for approximately 200 years. These four nations were given their independence in 1948.

Lioness, the (or Lion): One of the four beasts depicted in Daniel 7; believed to be Great Britain.

Lions, Strong (or Young): The strongest nations that came out of the former British Empire, believed to be Canada, New Zealand, Australia, and the United States of America.

Little Horn: A term used by Daniel to refer to the Beast.

Maastricht Treaty: A treaty signed by the Council of Ministers of the EU in the city of Maastricht, the Netherlands, in 1991. The purpose of the treaty was to create a monetary union in Europe by January 1, 1999, and later a political union. This treaty is the basis of all the other European treaties, including the Lisbon Treaty.

Magog: Son of Japheth, the eldest son of Noah; thought to have settled in the region of the Scythians, now southern Russia.

Marriage Supper (of the Lamb): A time after the rapture when Jesus celebrates His wedding to the redeemed as His bride.

Mecca: Birthplace of Mohammed; a holy city of Islam.

Medina: Site of Mohammed's tomb; a holy city of Islam.

Medo-Persia: Darius the Mede conquered the Neo-Babylonian Empire and thus combined the areas of the Medes and the Persians. This all took place during the time of Daniel.

Michael: The archangel, protector of the children of Israel; the "restrainer" of 2 Thessalonians 2:6–7.

Millennium: One thousand years. The millennial kingdom of Christ will come after the battle of Armageddon.

Moab: Incestuous son of Lot (his tribe settled on the east side of the Jordon); a part of the modern nation of Jordan.

Mother/son religion: Occult pagan religion of the Middle East starting shortly after the Noahic flood.

Mystery Babylon: Believed to be the Roman Catholic Church.

Nations: Refers to a kingdom, king, or horn.

Nebuchadnezzar: Chaldean king of Babylon who in 586 B.C. conquered Jerusalem, destroyed the Temple, and took the Jews captive into Babylon.

Nice Treaty: A refinement of the Maastricht Treaty.

North American Free Trade Agreement (NAFTA): A trade agreement between the United States, Canada, and Mexico.

Opt-outs: Certain sections of the Maastricht Treaty that were made non-compliant for Great Britain and Denmark.

Parousia: A Greek word meaning the "presence or coming" of an important person. This word is used of Jesus' second coming.

Pax: Latin for "peace." Commonly used in conjunction with *Pax Romana,* which refers to the long period of relative peace enforced by the Roman Empire from 27 B.C. to 180 A.D.

Pergamos: An ancient city in Asia Minor; Satan's throne during John the Apostle's time.

persecution, the: Popularly known as the tribulation of the Beast, which will take place at the beginning of the second half of the seven years and end before the end of the seven years.

Prostitute, the: Believed to be the Roman Catholic Church (also known as Mystery Babylon).

Rapture: The catching up of all those who have trusted Jesus for their salvation into the sky. This event takes place on the same day (though slightly before) the wrath of God falls.

Single European Act: A treaty signed in Rome in 1987 by the then twelve members of the European Union. This treaty brought about the European Single Market of January 1, 1992.

Temple: The most holy site in all Israel that can only be built on Mount Moriah (better known as the Temple Mount in Jerusalem).

Ten-horn(ed) beast: Ten European nations that Scripture says form the revived Roman Empire. These ten nations fulfill Revelation 17:12–13. They are also seen as the toes of the image of Daniel 2 and the fourth beast of Daniel 7:7.

Third Temple: The Temple built during Daniel's last seven-year period.

Two Witnesses: Two prophets who will operate in the power of God in an astounding manner.

BIBLIOGRAPHY

Alnor, William M. *Soothsayers of the Second Advent*. Old Tappan, NJ: Power Books, 1989.

Amplified Bible, adapted note from the *Homiletic Commentary* and the *Commentary on the Whole Bible* by Jamison, Fausset, and Brown published by Zondervan Publishers.

Bloomfield, Arthur. *Before the Last Battle—Armageddon*. Minneapolis, MN: Bethany House Publishers, 1971.

——. *The End of Days*. Minneapolis, MN: Bethany House Publishers, 1961.

Breese, Dave. *Europe and the Prince That Shall Come*. Hillboro, KS: Christian Destiny, n.d.

Bullock, Randy. *The Appointed Times*. Cheshire, UK: Tony MacCormack Publishers, 1996.

Chandler, Russell. *Doomsday*. Ann Arbor, MI: Servant Publishers, 1993.

Cooper, Charles. *Fight, Flight, or Faith*. Bellefonte, PA: Strong Tower Publishers, 2008.

Dolan, David. *Holy War for the Promised Land*. Nashville, TN: Thomas Nelson, 1991.

Dyer, Charles H. *The Rise of Babylon*. Wheaton, IL: Tyndale House Publishers, 1991.

Europe magazine excerpts, used with permission of *Europe* magazine. Subscriptions are $19.95 per year, 2100 M. Street, N.W., 7th floor, Washington, D.C. 20037.

Feinberg, Charles L. *The Minor Prophets*. Chicago, IL: Moody Press, 1976.

———. *Focus on Prophecy*. Old Tappan, NJ: Fleming Revell Publishers, 1964.

Frommer, Arthur. *Frommer's Belgium*. New York: Prentice Hall, 1984.

Goetz, William R. *The Economy to Come*. Alberta, Canada: Horizon House Publishers, 1983.

Grant, Charles. *Delors: Inside the House Jacques Built*. London, UK: Nicholas Brealey Publishers, 1994.

Gumerlock, Francis X. *The Day and the Hour*. Atlanta, GA: American Vision, 2000.

Hocking, David. *Dare to be a Daniel*, vol. 1 and 2. Orange, CA: Promise Publishers, 1991.

Hunt, Dave. *Global Peace*. Eugene, OR: Harvest House Publishers, 1990.

Hutchings, Noah. *Daniel*. Oklahoma City, OK: Hearthstone Publishers, 1990.

———. *The Revived Roman Empire and the Beast of the Apocalypse*. Oklahoma City, OK: Hearthstone Publishers, 1993.

James, William T. *Storming Toward Armageddon*. Green Forest, AZ: New Leaf Press Inc., 1992.

Jamison, Fausset, and Brown. *Commentary on the Whole Bible*. Grand Rapids, MI: Zondervan Publishing House, 1961.

Jeffrey, Grant R. *The Prince of Darkness*. Toronto, Canada: Frontier Research Publications, 1994.

Jeremiah, David. *Escape the Coming Night*. Dallas TX: Word Publishing, 1990.

Johnian, Mona. *Life in the Millennium*. South Plainsfield, NJ: Bridge Publishers, 1992.

La Haye, Tim, and Jerry B. Jenkins. *Are We Living in the Last Times?* Wheaton, IL: Tyndale House Publishers, 1999.

——. *The Beginning of the End*. Wheaton, IL: Tyndale House Publishers, 1972.

——. *How to Study the Bible for Yourself*. Eugene, OR: Harvest House Publishers, 1990.

——. *Revelation*. Grand Rapids, MI: Zondervan Publishing House, 1979.

Larkin, Clarence. *Dispensational Truth*. Philadelphia, PA: Clarence Larkin Estates Publisher, 1920.

——. *Rightly Dividing the Word*. Glenside, PA: Clarence Larkin Estates Publisher, n.d.

Larson, David. *Jews, Gentiles and the Church*. Grand Rapids, MI: Discovery House Publishers, 1995.

Lindsey, Hal. *The Late Great Planet Earth*. Grand Rapids, MI: Zondervan Publishing House, 1971.

——. *The Rapture*. New York: Bantam Books, 1983.

——. *Planet Earth—2000 A.D.* Palos Verdes, CA: Western Front Publishers, 1994.

——. *There's a New World Coming*. Eugene, OR: Harvest House Publishers, 1973.

Magee, J. Vernon. *Notes on Revelation*. Pasadena, CA: Thru the Bible Publishers, n.d.

McCall, Thomas S., and Zola Levitt. *The Coming Russian Invasion of Israel*. Chicago, IL: Moody Press, 1974.

Morris, Henry M. *The Revelation Record*. Grand Rapids, MI: Baker Books, 1976.

Noble, Charles F. *Drama of the Ages*. Glendale, CA: Church Press, 1955.

——. *Our Celestial Journey*. Glendale, CA: Church Press, 1957.

Otis, George Jr. *The Last of the Giants*. Tarrytown, NY: Chosen Books, 1991.

Pentecost, J. Dwight. *Will Man Survive?* Grand Rapids, MI: Lamplighter Books, 1990.

——. *Things to Come*. Grand Rapids, MI: Zondervan Publishing House, 1974.

Pettingill, William. *Bible Questions Answered*. Findley, OH: Durham Publishing House, 1958.

Price, Walter. *The Prophet Joel and the Day of the Lord.* Chicago, IL: Moody Press, 1976.

Robertson, Pat. *The New Millennium.* Waco, TX: Word Publishers, 1990.

Rogers, Adrian. *Unveiling The End Times in Our Times.* Nashville, TN: Broadman and Holman Publishers, 2004.

Richardson, Joel. *The Mideast Beast.* WND Books, Washington, D.C., 2012.

Rosenberg, Joel C. *The Twelfth Iman.* Wheaton, IL: Tyndale House Publishing, Inc., 2011.

Rosenberg, Joel C. *Epicenter.* Wheaton, IL: Tyndale House Publishing, Inc., 2006.

Rosenthal, Marvin J. *The Pre-Wrath Rapture of the Church.* Nashville, TN: Thomas Nelson, 1990.

Ryrie, Charles C. *The Ryrie Study Bible.* Chicago, IL: Moody Press, 1990.

———. *The Final Countdown.* Wheaton, IL: Victor Books, 1991.

Scofield, C. I. *The Scofield Reference Bible.* New York: Oxford University Press, 1909.

Sevener, Harold A. *God's Man in Babylon.* Charlotte, NC: Chosen People Ministries, 1994.

Smith, Chuck. *What the World is Coming To.* Costa Mesa, CA: The Word for Today, 1977.

Stewart, Don, and Chuck Missler. *The Coming Temple.* Orange, CA: Dart Press, 1991.

Strass, Lehman. *God's Plan for the Future.* Grand Rapids, MI: Zondervan Publishing House, 1965.

Thiessen, Henry C. *Introductory Lectures in Systematic Theology.* Grand Rapids, MI: William B. Eerdmans Publishers, 1963.

Tracy, Edward H. *Babylon the Great Is Fallen, Is Fallen.* San Francisco, CA: Published by author, 1960.

Van Impe, Jack. *Revelation Revealed.* Mount Pleasant, MI: Enterprise Printers Inc., 1982.

Van Kampen, Robert. *The Rapture Question Answered.* Grand Rapids, MI: Fleming H. Revell, 1997.

———. *The Sign.* Wheaton, IL: Crossway Books, 1992.

Walvoord, John F. *The Rapture Question*. Grand Rapids, MI: Zondervan Publishing House, 1957.

Walvoord, John F., and John E. Armageddon, *Oil and the Middle East Crisis*. Grand Rapids, MI: Zondervan Publishing House, 1974.

Walvoord, John F., and Roy Zuck. Wheaton, IL: *The Bible Knowledge Commentary, New Testament Edition*, 1983.

White, John W. *Re-Entry*. Grand Rapids, MI: Zondervan Publishing House, 1970.

Author Contact

The author is available for speaking engagements,
seminars, conferences, or questions.
He may be contacted by
email at inourrig@gmail.com

To order additional copies of this book,
please visit www.redemption-press.com
Available on Amazon.com and BarnesandNoble.com
Or call toll free 1 (844) 2REDEEM (273-3336)

CPSIA information can be obtained at www.ICGtesting.com
Printed in the USA
LVOW12s1447140615

442425LV00011B/566/P